HOW WOULD CONFUCIUS ASK FOR A RAISE?

Other Books by Carol Orsborn

Enough Is Enough: Simple Solutions for Complex People
Inner Excellence: Spiritual Principles of Life-Driven Business

HOW WOULD CONFUCIUS ASK FOR A RAISE?

100

ENLIGHTENED SOLUTIONS FOR TOUGH BUSINESS PROBLEMS

CAROL ORSBORN

WILLIAM MORROW AND COMPANY, INC.

NEW YORK

It is the policy of William Morrow and Company, Inc., and its imprints and affiliates, recognizing the importance of preserving what has been written, to print the books we publish on acid-free paper, and we exert our best efforts to that end.

Library of Congress Cataloging-in-Publication Data

Orsborn, Carol.
    How would Confucius ask for a raise? : 100 enlightened solutions for tough
business problems / Carol Orsborn.
        p.   cm.
    ISBN 0-688-13074-7
    1. Career development.   2. Leadership.   3. Conduct of life.
4. Sociology, Confucian.   I. Title.
HF5381.O884   1994   93-46306
650.1—dc20   CIP

Printed in the United States of America

First Edition

1 2 3 4 5 6 7 8 9 10

BOOK DESIGN BY BRIAN MOLLOY

To my partner in business and in life, Dan Orsborn,
for giving me the gift of Nashville

The power of spiritual forces in the Universe—how active it is everywhere! Invisible to the eyes, and impalpable to the senses, it is inherent in all things, and nothing can escape its operation.

—Confucius

Contents

III. Managing Others   135

VI. Failure and Crisis   195

IX. Balance and Productivity   255

X. Inner Peace and Spiritual Practice 275

Appendices 307

Contributing Sources 319

Taking the Next Step . . . 329

Acknowledgments

He who walks in truth and is devoted in his thinking, and furthermore reveres the worthy, is blessed by heaven.

—Confucius

To my agent, Patti Breitman
To my editor, Adrian Zackheim
To my children, Jody and Grant Orsborn
To my parents, Lloyd and Mae Matzkin
To my friends in Marin County, San Francisco, and Nashville
To my teachers and colleagues at Vanderbilt University Divinity School

You have my deepest gratitude and appreciation.

Author's Note

Clients of The Orsborn Group Public Relations, Inc., and members of the Society for Inner Excellence, have contributed case histories and anecdotal support for the principles shared in this book. When requested, I have honored their desire for anonymity by changing personal and company names and fictionalizing details.

Preface

On the very day I finished my response to the hundredth tough business problem in this book, I found myself lost on a freeway somewhere in my new hometown, Nashville, in the midst of the most severe thunder and lightning storm I have ever encountered. With a carful of people, the responsibility to stay calm through the violent weather was enormous. Even though I longed to stop driving, hide my head in my lap, and sob in terror, I did not have that option. Instead I struggled to keep my vehicle—not to mention my breathing—under control. Despite windows that suddenly fogged and navigational landmarks that vanished behind sheets of rain, I somehow managed to maneuver my little white Saturn through the electrical field that flashed, crashed, and miraculously rolled me back in the direction of my new house.

Only much later, tucked into bed, did I remember that one year ago, just before starting this book, I had received an omen about this day—an omen that foretold the spiritual challenges I would face during the course of this endeavor. I remembered in particular four little words:

Oh, oh!

Ha, ha!

When I thought of the omen's words, the fears that I had brought to my bed with me—not only from this day of lightning and thunder but from a year's worth of disruption—melted away in peals of relieved laughter. Suddenly I understood that I had somehow muddled my way through yet another round of life's challenges, as I had done so many times since meeting my spiritual teacher.

I remembered the words of the omen so vividly because they came to me on the very day that I asked my teacher for guidance on the advisability of writing the book you now hold in your hands. As I approached with my heartfelt inquiry, I felt only the deepest gratitude that I had a teacher who was always willing and able to guide me through the day-to-day challenges of my life. For many years I had hoped that such a teacher would appear to me. I took many courses and seminars, sat at the foot of many a guru, hoping that one or another would draw me in and keep me for good. Although each one contributed valuable lessons, wisdom that continues to benefit me every day, somehow I always found myself back on the curb again.

Throughout the decades of my search I sought comfort in a well-worn book with yellow covers that I kept by the side of my bed. Each time I consulted the book, I received an expanded understanding of the situation I faced, the part I played, and the best course of action to move me forward on my spiritual path.

The book was the *I Ching* or *Book of Changes*, translated by Richard Wilhelm, a three-thousand-year-old guide to life loaned to me by a dormmate during a bout with mononucleosis that hit me midway through my junior year of college. A student at the University of California–Berkeley, I had been overwhelmed by the social and political turbulence of the winter of 1969 and had sought temporary refuge at the University of California's Santa Cruz campus. But instead of finding refuge, I lay ill in my dorm, feeling increasingly alone and alienated.

The illness came at a moment when I felt the world of my childhood—and in those turbulent times it sometimes felt like the universe itself—coming unhinged. I was several years and thousands of miles away from the comforts and traditions of my Jewish upbringing in Chicago, unwilling to admit defeat by calling home for help. Clearly this illness had catapulted me headfirst into the initiatory crisis of my budding adulthood.

As I lay there, many of the life issues that would initiate and fuel my spiritual search for decades to follow were taking form in my feverish brain. For example, I had written a letter to the publisher of the *Chicago Daily News*, a man who had mentored me during my summer internship as a reporter there. I had begged for the offer of a permanent job at the paper from him. I now wiped my brow with the letter he sent back to me. Though my mentor preferred that I finish my degree, he would take me on now if I really felt it was the right thing to do.

26

Should I leave school and take the position? In view of the world's need for help here and now, was the time I was spending in college studying the past, and honing my thinking skills simply intellectual self-indulgence? Was my illness punishment for this transgression? How was I to help make this a better world? How could I quench the yearning I felt in every fiber of my being for a relationship with the universe that would make sense of my life?

The book with the yellow cover beckoned to me. I opened it at random and began reading.

I soon learned that over three thousand years ago those who would be leaders also grappled with the issue of how best to make their contribution to the world. Enriched by the stories of my ancient predecessors, my question about whether or not to stay in college deepened into the philosophical quandary that has challenged those who have come before me for at least three thousand years: Which is the better path? To throw oneself into the world with hopes of changing it—or to remove oneself from the battlefield of daily life to develop one's character?

Eagerly I soaked up the tales of leaders who marshaled their forces and marched into battles to fight for issues they deeply believed in. They didn't always win. Sometimes it was character traits that did them in—arrogance or impatience. Sometimes it was immutable fate. Sometimes they decided that the wisest course was not to fight at all, or to find the perfect moment to retreat. They recovered to try again— or they transcended the mainstream of everyday life to develop themselves further.

Through it all, the seasons changed. Nature withheld its rain, or burst forth to nurture the land. Foxes drowned in swollen rivers. White horses came as if on wings. Birds descended to their nests.

At first skipping haphazardly through the vivid images, sometimes put off by terminology that offended my contemporary feminist sensibilities, often having not the foggiest idea what the poetic language and cryptic phrases found in those readings meant in the context of my life, I was fascinated by it all. But increasingly I realized that the *I Ching* was playing in the ballpark where answers to my bigger questions would be found.

Before long I was tempted out of my sickbed to throw three Chinese coins on my dormitory floor, their seemingly random patterns of falling heads and tails surprisingly leading me more precisely to appropriate passages to read and contemplate.

As the book's imagery began to make more and more sense to me, I recognized that the guidance I was receiving daily was as often challenging as it was comforting. Refusing to respond with simplistic yes-or-no answers, the *I Ching* continually turned my inquiries back to me, forcing me to walk the spiritual path that would be uniquely mine.

For example, when I first inquired about whether my urge to stay in school—developing myself inwardly rather than moving to take on an active role in the world—was self-indulgent, I was given the image of a man trying to hunt in a strange forest without a guide. The *I Ching* explained, "He loses his way. When he finds himself in difficulties he must not try to steal out of them unthinkingly and without guidance. Fate cannot be duped; premature effort, without the necessary guidance, ends in failure and disgrace."

When I first read this passage, I felt a shiver of recognition as I saw myself as the hunter lost in the woods. Without adequate support my desire to leave school at this point to make a greater contribution to the world was sheer escapist fantasy. The truth is that I was not even handling very well the challenges that were already on my plate. To try to accomplish something great at this point would be premature and lead to failure.

Should I stay in school? I cast the coins again—and got the same exact reading. What are the probabilities of that happening two times in a row? Playfully, testing, I cast them again—and once again they came up in the same combination of heads and tails.

When I went to cast them a fourth time, I was led to a new reading. This one scolded me for my obtusiveness, informing me that "if mistrustful or unintelligent questioning is kept up, it serves only to annoy the teacher. He does well to ignore it in silence, just as the oracle gives one answer only and refuses to be tempted by questions implying doubt."

The next several times I cast the coins, the answers were completely unintelligible to me.

Finally, feeling contrite, I accepted the *I Ching*'s commentary on the subject at hand: "A certain measure of taking oneself in hand, brought about by strict discipline, is a good thing.''

At last I got the message. I responded to the offer of a job at the newspaper by writing my mentor and telling him that I had decided to stick it out at school through graduation.

First there had been the shock of self-recognition: the admission of my youthful arrogance. Oh, oh. Then there was the relief of having been freed from illusion, able to stay on the path that, regardless of how convoluted it appeared to me at the time, was actually the fastest and most efficient way to fulfill my destiny. Ha, ha!

And so began the ongoing dialogue that led me to explore and discover fascinating new facets of my life. When, for instance, I finally graduated college, eager to save the world, and settled instead for my first job as an associate editor at the *San Francisco Chronicle*, the *I Ching* mercifully slowed the pace of my restless ambition by teaching that ''whatever endures can be created only gradually by long-continued work and careful reflection.''

While my career path apparently continued to lead me farther and farther away from my idealistic urgings—I founded a public relations agency that came to represent salami companies and insurance firms—the *I Ching* patiently stayed with me, showing me how to relate to my workplace as the arena for my spiritual growth.

When the subsequent success I experienced running the company threatened to take over my life, the *I Ching* gently reminded me of the dangers of deluded enthusiasm, guiding me back to balance and perspective.

Through these many years I had hoped and prayed for a teacher to come into my life to help me establish a relationship to the universe that would make sense of my life. At various times I suspected that it might come to me as a wise old woman in robes, a smart young therapist, or a sage workshop conductor in a three-piece suit. The *I Ching* counseled patience and persistence.

Recently in my career, when it became clear that the time was coming for me to leave the comfort of my role as businesswoman in order to take the leap to my new role as author and speaker, my desire for a teacher to emerge and present himself or herself to me peaked. I could not do this alone. As usual I went to my old friend, the *I Ching,* to ask how and when I would recognize my teacher. But before the coins ever left my hand, I recognized the irony of the moment.

Oh, oh.

Ha, ha.

Of course—this book was the very teacher I had sought for so many years. It had been right here beside me all along, every day of my adult life. Not only that but, guided by the *I Ching* all of these years, I was now prepared to share the wisdom I'd gained from our many sessions together in order to write a book for people in business.

And so it was, one year ago, that I sat down for a very serious session with the *I Ching*, asking for its judgment about my intention to present my interpretation of it in the form of this book. Here's what it said,

Shock brings success.
Shock comes—oh, oh!
Laughing words—ha, ha!
The shock terrifies for a hundred miles,
And he does not let fall the sacrificial spoon and chalice.

The commentary elaborated,

When a man has learned within his heart what fear and trembling mean, he is safeguarded against any terror produced by outside influences. Let the thunder roll and spread terror a hundred miles around; he remains so composed and reverent in spirit that the sacrificial rite is not interrupted. This is the spirit that must animate leaders and rulers of men—a profound inner seriousness from which all outer terrors glance off harmlessly.

I felt enlivened by the challenge the *I Ching* posed—to write a book with the energy of creativity bursting forth from the heavens like lightning and thunder, to engage in this process while maintaining a profound inner seriousness from which all outer terrors would glance off harmlessly.

As it turned out, the span of time it took to write this book has coincided with what has been the most tumultuous period of my life to date—a period that would make my feverish deliberations about whether or not to stay in school several decades ago seem mild by comparison.

For several years, largely through the faith and support of my husband-partner, Dan, I had been able to devote myself more fully to my writing and teaching. Business and spirituality have merged into one whole—the issues of inner conflict between my ambition and my spirit initiated during my college years coming to resolution at long last. One would hope to live happily ever after.

However, not long after I received the contract to write this, my third book, Dan was inspired to pursue his lifelong dream of finding a way to integrate the separate spheres of *his* life into one whole as well; in his case it was business and country music. In short he proposed to move our family from our home of several decades, Marin County, California, to Nashville, Tennessee.

Would I rise to the occasion, finding it within myself to be as supportive of Dan's urge for integration as he had been of mine? Would I find a way to give our children the support they would need to make a stable transition to their new schools and environment? Would I be able to keep my wits about me through this process, not only handling the logistics of the move—but simultanously managing the writing of this book? Was, as the *I Ching* forewarned, holding on to my sacrificial spoon through the terrifying shock to involve not only giving up my settled life in Mill Valley, bringing nearly superhuman discipline to carve out the time and energy I needed to write this book, but the greatest sacrifice of all: watching cherished notions of myself as a loving, supportive person—a person of faith—severely challenged over and over again during this year of transition?

I could not resist finding out. And so, all the while writing this book, I have been engaged in the wrenching process of leaving behind our Mill Valley home and initiating our new life in Nashville.

As part of this process, we turned over the reins of our San Francisco office to our senior staff, knowing that we would have to let go of day-to-day management, surrendering to the process of transformation as the business reconfigures—painfully at times—around our new reality. Dan left early for Nashville to set up the fundamentals of our livelihood while I, having sold our home, held some semblance of normal life together in Mill Valley, living and writing in a motel room as our children finished the school year.

Finally we joined Dan in Nashville, where I am now—surrounded by unpacked boxes and fresh paint—typing out these words.

I am inspired by a story Richard Wilhelm told in his 1923 preface to the *I Ching*. In the midst of World War I a group of Chinese scholars set up shop in an encampment outside the city of Tsingtao, then under heavy seige. Wilhelm, in charge of the Chinese Red Cross, used his free hours of relaxation to continue his studies of Chinese wisdom. As Wilhelm relates, "Happiest of all, however, was an old Chinese who was so wholly absorbed in his sacred books that not even a grenade falling at his side could disturb his calm. He reached out for it—it was a dud—then drew back his hand and, remarking that it was very hot, forthwith returned to his books."

The wild ride through shockwaves of lightning and thunder, holding on to my center of faith against the odds, on my last day of writing, was an appropriate conclusion to what this period of time has been about for me.

And what have I learned?

This I can summarize in four little words.

Oh, oh!

Ha, ha!

—Carol Orsborn
Nashville, TN

Introduction

In the words and deeds of the past there lies hidden treasure that men may use to strengthen and elevate their own characters. The way to study the past is not to confine oneself to mere knowledge of history but, through application of this knowledge, to give actuality to the past.

—The *I Ching*

Today's business people have unprecedented access to spiritual principles from ages and cultures that not long ago would have been revered as "secret knowledge." Historically this secret knowledge was used for serious business—to fight and win wars, to build financial and political dynasties, and to accumulate power, wealth, and sometimes even the greatest prize of all: inner peace.

Although we can walk into any esoteric bookstore in the country and purchase the books bearing the wisdom of these sacred scrolls, we have seen that it's one thing to have access to these principles—and quite another to apply them to one's work life.

Happily a rapidly growing number of business people around the world have taken the time to crack the mysterious codes, forging ahead with the application of spiritual principles in their own careers and companies. They are fueled by the grassroots realization, simultaneously emerging on many levels of Western society—from individuals grappling with the meaning of success in their lives to institutions impacted by changing times—that the old paradigm of business-as-usual no longer works for us. As the tone and results of the 1992 American presidential election demonstrated, people are desperate for change. And an increasing number of us are willing to put our very perception of reality on the line for it.

This is no idle statement—for it is indeed in our very perception of reality that the change from old to new paradigm takes root.

In Willis Harman and John Hormann's seminal book, *Creative Work: The Constructive Role of Business in a Transforming Society*, the authors follow numerous historical strands in Western culture, from postmedieval society through modern times, to reveal and explain many of the core beliefs we have unwittingly inherited and applied in our work lives.

For instance they point to the modernization movement of the seventeenth century—the emergence of the rationalists and the realization that the sun and not the earth was the center of the cosmos—as a profound shift. It was a shift in world-view from one in which the universe and all its creatures are interconnected in a "Great Chain of Being," to a more fragmented view of the world, in which the natural resources of the earth were seen as being put here for mankind's use. The contemporary expression of this materialistic point of view is our alienation from nature, our putting individual prosperity before the care and preservation of earth's life-support systems. At present many contemporary businesses are operating with such a low level of ecological awareness that the very survival of our planet is threatened.

Another related strand of the old paradigm, one that has been influencing society for over five thousand years, is the patriarchal model, enshrining arbitrary power in a male parental model which finds contemporary expression in the traditional church establishment, the concept of the nation-state, and the modern corporation.

The patriarchal model derives from a basically negative view of human nature; it assumes that the stability of society requires that humans be controlled by some sort of external and hierarchical authority. This aspect of old-paradigm thinking expresses itself today in organizations that depend on accepted dogma, excessive bureacracy, and a reliance on external expertise and authority—undercutting the individual's ability to act independently and spontaneously. This fuels the epidemic of burnout and stress that plagues the corporate environment today as poor workforce morale undermines not only the well-being of workers but the corporation's bottom line.

There's more: The scientific revolution's technological approach to problem solving, which has unwittingly moved the locus of individual meaning from spiritual solutions such as acceptance and transcendence inspired by faith to invention and consumerism as a way of dealing with discomfort and pain. This has led to a reactive approach to problem solving that attempts to relieve symptoms rather than cure causes.

The convergence of these various strands explains our contemporary work ethic—a largely self-destructive belief system built upon the old-paradigm premise that if you work hard and are smart enough, you can control your environment, either by solving every conceivable problem through science and technology or by purchasing the goods and services you require to eliminate discomfort.

Fortunately just as painful awareness of the impact of fragmented thinking in our lives and society is bubbling to the surface, other, more positive strands of history are converging—seemingly just in the nick of time—into a new paradigm.

The new paradigm is based on the alternative belief that there is a greater unity and connectedness between ourselves as individuals—and our careers, countries, planet, and universe—than we have allowed ourselves to experience in the West for several centuries. Ironically the same scientific methods that contributed to the fragmentation of our knowledge and understanding of the world are now leading us back to appreciate the interrelationship between heaven and earth. We can see that hairspray applied in France eats a hole in the ozone layer over Antarctica; that trees burned in Brazil alter the weather patterns in North America.

Exploring our connectedness on an even more intimate level, scientist-philosophers such as Deepak Chopra, M.D., author of *Ageless Body, Timeless Mind,* demonstrate that the very air we breathe contains molecules that have circulated through the bodies of every living organism who came before us. From Julius Caesar to Marco Polo, from Diogenes to Dr. Martin Luther King, there is increasing scientific evidence that we are indeed one.

Simultaneously those scientists who turned their attention to the human dimension contributed the paradigm-busting realization that the human mind and spirit has far more potential and depth—not to mention commonality—than had previously been supposed. Consider Sigmund Freud's discovery of the multiple levels of human consciousness, and Carl Jung's identification of the collective unconscious.

Finally, science and technology have fueled an information explosion, giving scholars and retailers alike the high-tech tools to crack and disseminate the secrets contained in faded fragments of ancient works, providing access to philosophical and spiritual paradigms from other cultural traditions. Sacred texts, teachings, and rituals from places such as India, Africa, Tibet, and China have opened our eyes and hearts to a world of expanded possibilities—a new way of relating to the world, ourselves, and each other.

As the new paradigm unfolds, we see a shift not only in how our companies are run—traditional hierarchies replaced by decentralized power and debureaucratization, for example—but, at a second, even grander level, we are experiencing a rethinking of how our very economy functions. There is movement toward use of more appropriate technology and proactive environmental action, there is greater appreciation of our connection and responsibility to developing countries, and much more.

Operating on a third level—the interpersonal—new-paradigm thinking leads us from models of domination to those of partnership as we explore the possibilities for respectful and loving relationships not only in our immediate families but in the workplace.

But it is on a fourth level—the personal—that I believe the truly transformative work of the new paradigm takes place. This is the level that must be fully and individually addressed before any important work on the previously described three levels can truly take root. Harman and Hormann describe proponents of this fourth approach as "those who perceive the problems to be rooted in the essential or conditioned nature of human beings, and so call for new ways of being."

This new way of being is the key to change, what management consultant Peter Senge, author of *The Fifth Discipline*, refers to as intrinsic rather than extrinsic motivation.

Referring to my concept of inner excellence, Senge explains,

Many managers are seeking to build 'the new organization' that can learn and adapt in the age of interdependence and continual change. The irony is that many will try and few will succeed, for the very reason that building this organization purely as a reaction to external challenges is unlikely to generate the commitment required to succeed. . . . That commitment can only come from having the deep desire of people to truly work together in a new and different way.

What is this new way of being? The groundwork has been laid by philosophers, spiritual leaders, psychologists, activists, visionaries, and futurists, who have introduced, demonstrated, and legitimized the empowering belief that once out of the shadow of the old paradigm, human beings are eager to give expression to their basic goodness. We reinvent our relationships, our workplaces, and our economies out of the conviction that we are connected to one another in ways that expand the concept of community to include the entire universe. We discover that we have the right and the ability to tune in to our own inner wisdom and to recognize and act on universal truths greater than, yet encompassing, ourselves, giving our innate urge to express and fulfill our potential as human beings precedence over arbitrary external authority. We have the ability to take courageous action on behalf of ourselves and for each other.

Reunited with a sense of a whole greater than ourselves, we are freed from the arrogant illusion that we stand alone in the universe, just one technological breakthrough away from controlling our destinies. With newfound humility we recognize the need for and reclaim our right to a relationship with the universe that helps us make sense of our lives. We are willing to leave the realm of the merely mechanistic and rational and begin to explore the mysteries of our new frontier: the interior of our own hearts.

This is the realm of spirituality, that deeply alive place within each of us that longs for fulfillment.

This is the level where concepts such as faith, compassion, forgiveness, acceptance, and surrender transcend old-paradigm rationalism to become useful tools for us—not only when we ask questions about the meaning and purpose of our lives but also when we address the practical issues confronting us each and every day as we go about our work.

This is the level at which an ever-growing number of business people are beginning to operate. They are learning how to tap inner resources that allow them to make better business decisions, to find the most creative solutions, and to inspire those with whom they work. From a computer technology firm that institutes ''mental health days''

and sabbaticals—and watches profitability soar—to a corporate secretary who finds the courage to leave her job and start a thriving
entrepreneurial venture in the field of her dreams, a growing number
of us are coming to understand that there need be no discrepancy
between spirituality and success in the workplace. In fact more and
more of us have come to know that it is from our most deeply held
beliefs that our greatest success can come.

Seen from this new perspective, the true task of the individual is
to rise to his or her own highest level of development as a human
being, inspiring others to do the same. This is real leadership, a definition for a new way of being that applies to the empowered individual regardless of whether or not he or she holds external authority
over others.

My new definition of leadership has its personal roots in the mid-
eighties. At that time—well into the second decade of my career—I
found myself asking why I, like so many of my peers in business,
was feeling so unfulfilled. It wasn't that my career wasn't progressing,
that my company wasn't growing; I had referral networks and support
systems to equal my good reputation. But business always seemed to
take more from me than it gave back. Seventy-hour weeks, once the
province of the exceptionally inspired or driven, had, for me and my
contemporaries, become the norm.

It was no longer an option for me to meet the challenges I was
facing by trying any harder, working any longer, or striving for more
excellence—the only solutions offered by the American management
mainstream. I was already at the limit. It was clear to me that I would
have to stop urging myself and my employees on to increasingly self-
destructive heights and instead try something new.

I tapped this underground of discontent in the mid-eighties with
the publication of *Enough Is Enough*, the handbook for Overachievers
Anonymous. An organization for people who were already too busy,
the group attracted fifteen thousand members on a platform promising
''no meetings, no classes, and no fund-raisers.'' The group continues
under our new name: the Society for Inner Excellence.

Enough Is Enough was among the first books to encourage people
juggling the multiple balls of career, family, and quality of life to
question the myth of ''having it all'' and begin to make tough but
necessary choices. I contended that the problems that we faced daily

could not simply be answered by another book on time management, prioritization, or coping. There had to be something more—something that would transform rather than simply manipulate the system.

At that time my husband and I, our firm's principals, cut back our hours at work to make the time and space for personal exploration of alternatives. Fully expecting to pay for the reclamation of time in our lives by being poor, we reduced the size of our company and moved from our "dream house" to a more modest cottage.

But to our surprise our brush with downward mobility proved to be short-lived. In fact, without sacrificing any of our newfound values, business boomed. Within three years we were back to handling our previous billings while spending substantially fewer hours at work. While we and our staff were busy, we were no longer burning out.

Our search for alternatives had taken us off the beaten path and onto the exploration of new terrain. For guidance we had turned from traditional business-management books to alternative sources of inspiration—everything from myth to esoteric literature, from folklore to history.

We began increasingly to realize that the tough business problems all of us face in our day-to-day lives have solutions rooted not only in the mundane but in the spiritual realm. For instance, I began to realize that trying to satisfy unfair and demanding clients was not only a reflection of their abuse of authority over me but was also an issue of my lack of faith that something better would come along if I found the courage to resign the account. We began to approach all the situations we faced in business as if there were more to them than we had been trained to perceive and respond to . . . a spiritual dimension. No longer was our work life the battlefield where success was the prize to be won for sacrificing ourselves for our careers, but rather the arena where success was experienced as the nurturing and growth of our spirits, regardless of our results at any given time.

Though more and more is being written about the need to apply spiritual principles in the business environment, we often have little idea of what spirituality looks and feels like—and how actually to apply it in the arena of our daily lives. Even those of us who have been well schooled in religious or spiritual practices find ourselves hesitant to apply what we know in the "real world," particularly in the arena of our livelihood, where matters of survival are at stake.

This book is an attempt to help close this gap.

Before I delve into the heart of this book, I must begin with a disclaimer. I do not believe that business is the appropriate environment for talking about and teaching spiritual principles. Rather I believe that the business environment is the place where one *acts* from one's inner convictions. The leader's job is not to teach his or her subordinates about the principles I will be outlining in this book but rather to live from and by them, inspiring others by example.

This is the path I have walked for twenty-four years. Through the decades my consistent guide on the spiritual path has been the *I Ching*, a book of wisdom from ancient China that dates back over three thousand years. The book has had a profound influence on how I have run my business and my career.

For decades many Westerners have shared my fascination with the promise of knowledge contained in the classic yellow volume that resides on many an executive's bookshelf. But even in the inspired Richard Wilhelm translation, much of the *I Ching*'s rich wisdom is cloaked in esoteric language and symbolism more suited to the serious student than to the business person looking for pressing answers.

Those of us who have invested the time are finding the *I Ching* to be strikingly applicable to today's workplace challenges. Some of us have been connected, along with scholars and academics from around the world, through *The I Ching Network,* a newsletter established in 1985 by Professor Kidder Smith of Bowdoin College, Department of Asian Studies, which exists to exchange information among researchers on the *I Ching* as well as to explore the contemporary relevance of the *I Ching* and its practical application. A recent issue of *Network*, sharing the results of a Nexus search, reports that instruction in the *I Ching* has formed part of IBM's in-house training course called "Fit for the Future." More than six hundred employees have attended the course over a five-year period. I have quoted the *I Ching* to rapt corporate audiences of employees ranging from Apple Computer to Prudential Insurance, and introduced its concepts to professionals, tradespeople, individuals working for huge companies such as AT&T and start-up entrepreneurs with one-person shops, and have found a growing willingness to consider new approaches to old problems.

What makes the *I Ching* so valuable to people in the workplace today is its universal applicability to approaching life issues. The wisdom it offers is not dogmatic but rather process oriented.

The *I Ching* does not contend that there is one right response for everyone, under every circumstance. Additionally the *I Ching* makes no effort to displace individual traditions and spiritual legacies that may be important to the querent. In fact the book guides its students to honor and respect their ancestors—a concept I have come to interpret as including the particular religious tradition to which they have been born.

As Carol K. Anthony paradoxically states in her book, *The Philosophy of the I Ching,* "There is no such thing as a philosophy of the *I Ching*. It is no system of belief, nor is it a systematized explanation of our existence." Rather the *I Ching* gently guides querents on their own individual search for meaning by helping them tap into the depths of their own intuitive awareness. Inner awareness, when not obstructed by alienating character traits such as fear, impatience, and greed, connects the individual to universal truths, recognizable on a gut level.

Anthony, using imagery taken directly from the *I Ching,* describes this as "the universality of truth that lies like a water table under all the wells of a community. This universal truth exists in everyone in the form of their intuitive and unconscious knowledge. It is a sort of lowest common denominator which applies equally to everyone."

These universal truths express themselves in the language of the *I Ching* as "Tao," the Unifying Principle that brings order out of chaos, meaning out of the void, harmony out of discord.

The Chinese character for the word *Tao* portrays a foot guided by a head. The foot represents the rational, intellectual capabilities that prevail in today's corporate environment—the concern with action in the outer world that has dominated our Western cultural tradition for so many centuries. The head represents intuition and inner wisdom, spiritual approaches and traits more fully developed in non-Western traditions.

It takes both qualities to comprise the Tao—and they must be in healthy balance. But it is important to note that progress depends on the head leading the foot: we must honor our own intuition, our inner knowing, even above our rational, intellectual capabilities.

Having been shaped by the teachings of the *I Ching,* I look to the larger picture—accessing and sharing universal wisdom from the many spiritual traditions that have had an impact on me over the years—to build a bridge between the imagery of the ancient Chinese work and our own Western heritage. In writing this book, when I felt drawn to alternative sources for imagery and inspiration, I let myself follow my impulse, sometimes to destinations that surprised even me.

However, before I felt sufficiently empowered to bring this level of creativity to this project, I had a major hurdle to overcome. Confucius, the ancient Chinese philosopher whose ideas I was introduced to through my studies of the *I Ching*, has had a profound influence on wisdom through the ages. Without academic degrees, official position, or divine declaration, who was I to think that I could bring anywhere near the same kind of wisdom to contemporary issues that he would have done?

However, my discomfort fortunately led me to learn more about the great philosopher and teacher, and it was what I learned about Confucius himself that contained the resolution I sought.

In Daniel J. Boorstin's book, *The Creators: A History of Heros of the Imagination*, I read that Confucius claimed no divine source for his teachings, nor any inspiration not open to everyone.

Confucius was never crucified, never martyred. He never led people out of a wilderness nor commanded forces in battle. He left little mark on the life of his time and aroused few disciples in his day. Pursuing the career of an ambitious reform-minded bureaucrat, he ended his life in frustration. It is easy to see him as an ancient Don Quixote. But his lifelong unsuccessful tilting against the evils of the chaotic Chinese states of his day somehow awakened his people, and eventually commanded two thousand years of Chinese culture.

Confucius did not believe himself to have access to information, insight, and wisdom not available to anyone willing to pursue the truth. He, too, turned to the *I Ching* as an important source of insight and guidance. He contemplated this work, applying its wisdom to the challenges he himself faced, offering his commentary based upon his experiences with it to the people of his day.

In extracting ten great notions from the *I Ching* that have been particularly important to me—which I will share with you in the "Executive Summary" that follows—as well as in responding to the "One Hundred Tough Business Problems" in Part Two of this book, I have attempted to live up to Confucius's definition of wisdom. According to Confucius, wisdom is the following: "When you know a thing, to recognize that you know it, and when you do not know a thing, to recognize that you do not know it."

My interpretation of the *I Ching* rests upon the philosophical base of my previous work, which reflects a broad range of spiritual influences, from Zen to Twelve Step materials, from my own Judeo-Christian heritage to Indian mysticism. In my previous works—most recently *Inner Excellence: Spiritual Principles of Life-Driven Business* (New World Library, 1993)—I shared this philosophical base with readers. Before I proceed with the "Executive Summary" of the *I Ching* I will summarize the essential components of the principles of inner excellence.

THE PRINCIPLES OF
INNER EXCELLENCE

SURRENDER

As we discussed earlier, we have inherited from postmedieval Western civilization a contemporary work ethic built upon the old-paradigm premise that if you work hard and smart enough, you can control the things that happen to you, thus eliminating pain and discomfort. This premise appears to be true as long as everything goes your way. However, the first time something goes wrong—as inevitably it will—the impetus to perform moves from inspiration to fear.

When you begin to learn to accept your human limitations, on the other hand, you stop being chased through worlds of ambition by the anxiety-driven belief that you could ever be good enough to control everything that happens to you. This is the principle of surrender.

When you stop wasting energy repressing negative possibilities, you have your complete potential available to you.

To illustrate this principle, let me tell you a personal story. I recall going to work after the opening shots of Desert Storm. The phones were quiet. In fact they were dead. No new business inquiries, no returned phone calls—nothing.

Traditionally January is a big month in our industry. In fact we depend on it to replace the business that tends to drop off at the end of each year. But that year we were going to see red ink creeping into our monthly accountings—something we hadn't seen for quite a while and had fervently hoped never to see again.

What to do? We surrendered. The course of the war—and its impact on our existing new business effort—was clearly beyond our control. Rather than damaging our spirits further, we called the staff together and conceded that this was not a time for new growth.

Instead we would consider this period a time of incubation—a time to implement some of those longer-range programs and plans we never seemed to have time for in the press of ordinary times. During this period Dan decided to become a major player in an area that held a lot of promise for the future—public relations for professional service firms. In fact he became national chairman of the Public Relations Society of America's Professional Services Section. Additionally, he took the opportunity to initiate the first and most successful local chapter in the country. Holding the staff together, believing as we did that someday the war would end and business resume, we assigned promotional projects on the subject of professional services—articles to be placed, brochures and booklets to be distributed. Eventually, when the cycle of doom and gloom lifted—as it always does—we were poised at a whole new level of public perception. In short order we picked up business—at advanced retainer levels—that more than made up for our losses during the war.

There is a difference between surrender and resignation. When you resign, you are admitting defeat to a hostile universe that is innately unfair and uncaring. When you surrender, however, you retain your belief that this is a loving universe and that the obstacles you face, while apparently steering you in a direction other than where it is you wish to go, are part of a bigger picture than you can yet understand. In other words, the difference between resignation and surrender is spiritual in nature. And what is the source of this spiritual quality?

FAITH

The ability to surrender comes from faith. If you believe that this is a universe that rewards and punishes, based on your "good" or "bad" behavior, you will be trapped in the old-paradigm performance model. You will not change how you practice leadership in your career or company until you change your beliefs about the nature of business and of life.

To have faith requires one to take the leap to a new belief: that the universe does not offer conditional rewards for good behavior. Rather, the universe supports you, no matter what—unconditionally, all the time, despite appearances to the contrary at any particular moment. In

45

the Judeo-Christian tradition we call this personal, loving force for good in one's life God.

Even if you feel doubtful that this is a loving universe, you can "act as if" it were true and get the same results. Assume that this is a universe that wants you to succeed, and you will find yourself more willing to take risks—be it in finding the courage to speak honestly, to be more authentic in the workplace, or to try to turn your ideas and aspirations into reality. You will know how to set limits and to protect yourself from those who would manipulate or abuse you.

These are attractive qualities—the essence of vitality. Job offers, new clients, and new opportunities are drawn to enthusiastic people— and it is no accident that the Latin root for the word *enthusiasm* means "to be filled with God."

COMPASSION

Faith enables you to extend to yourself the one quality that you need above all to be successful: compassion for your shortcomings. How quickly can you forgive yourself and find the courage to try again? Can you extend compassion to those who work for and with you? This is a key to leadership—the expression of spirituality that allows those around you to bring their best rather than their worst to work with themselves every day.

For many years we represented one of the country's leading restaurant groups. In promoting this company our job was to procure national exposure for them in the media. We reported to a demanding director of marketing, who set exceedingly high standards for us to meet week after week, month after month. Although he was tough, he was also fair.

After several years the marketing director was faced with an exciting career move. He had decided to leave his corporate home and take his life savings to open up the local franchise of a national fast-food operation. He asked us to be the agency.

We were thrilled, believing that our long relationship would translate to this new arena of challenge and opportunity. But there was a hitch. Now that it was his own money he was managing, he warned us that he could not afford for us to make any mistakes. Everything we did had to work the first time out—and work fast.

We pulled together the opening of openings—and in fact attracted the top local press to cover the event. We went to our next meeting following the exposure prepared for the pleasant exchange of pats on the back to which we'd become accustomed. Instead we sat face-to-face with a very glum client indeed.

The press had been great. But the hordes of happy customers he'd expected as a result had not shown up. We had done something very, very wrong—and we'd better do something to fix it. Today.

To make a long story short, we never came up with another great idea for him again. Fear had single-handedly wiped away years of camaraderie—the illusion of trust that we were all on the same team doing the best we could under the circumstances.

The spiritual alternative—the strategy that would have given both him and us the best chance of succeeding under these difficult circumstances—would have allowed us to fill in the gaps between reality and the results he preferred with faith, trust, and compassion. But our shortcomings were not forgiven by our client. As he was set suddenly adrift in a seemingly hostile universe, his own failures appeared to him as punishment. Devoid of compassion for himself and for those he retained, he quickly burned through several more competent agencies. Eventually he was forced to shut down his fast-food franchise.

RECEIVING

This client is typical of so many of us who believe we should have it within our power to make things turn out the way we'd like. We are seduced into giving everything we've got—and more. But the truth is that much of what we do is busy work, which accomplishes little more than deadening our spirits through exhaustion and fear. The harder we try, the farther away our goals seem to recede.

In order to stop "putting out" and start receiving, you will need to make a sacrifice. You must sacrifice the illusion that you can bribe fate with your good behavior—but you receive in return the gift of partnership with the universe.

When you can do this, you will flow into what's next for you. You won't need to push or control the outcome. You will find it in your

47

heart to sit patiently with complexity and imperfection without feeling compelled to find cursory resolution.

Letting go of your grandiose notions about yourself, you will regain clarity and perspective about yourself and what is really important to you. Out of true humility you will begin to see not only your faults and weaknesses but also the truth about your strengths and the ways you can contribute to the greater good as well. This is the key to fueling your ambition with inspiration rather than fear. This is the principle of receiving.

Illustrating this is the case of Robin, a friend in the high-pressure custom-clothing business, whose story I first related in *Inner Excellence*. During a particularly rough winter at the agency I got together with Robin for comfort. I told her that every January since I could remember, I dreaded the feeling that I was having to start over again in the new year by ''getting serious'' and ''making it happen.'' I was pushing myself to function as best I could under the circumstances—day after day. But the effort to perform was getting more and more unbearable.

She had an alarmingly simple solution: ''The next time you approach the front door of your business, ask yourself how you are feeling. If you feel fine, proceed. If you are freaking out, don't go in.''

Robin told me that she had once stood on the curb across the street from her store for over an hour, overwhelmed by the challenges she faced, not knowing where to begin. Normally she would have berated herself for her lack of enthusiasm—regaling herself with every failure—real or imagined, personal or professional—every character flaw.

But this day as she stood there, Robin gave herself permission to feel upset without the added judgment that being upset meant anything about her ability to do her job. While she was giving herself permission to have all of her feelings, she found herself wondering whether an important call she'd been waiting for had come in yet. She daydreamed about a certain sleeve that she felt the urge to sketch. She recognized that the combination of fabrics she saw on a woman as she passed by presented a simple solution to one of the knottier design challenges she faced. Robin practically *ran* across the street to work.

If you can find enough faith within yourself to stop pushing, you find that ''doing nothing'' is not always lost time. Its value is not only recuperative—although that would be benefit enough. By emptying yourself of fear-driven effort, you make the space to receive information, insight, and creative solutions not available through action-oriented behavior. You take the time to ponder, to appreciate, to daydream.

You surrender the arrogance of your controlled intellect to bask patiently in the world of obscured images, plans, and knowledge, which are pressing, as if of their own accord, to take shape. Trusting that larger forces than yourself are at work in your life, you will give up the demand for the outcome you think you want and learn to make room for surprises.

To learn to give up pushing and controlling, and to begin to let, surrender, and receive requires tremendous courage. How many of the long hours that you invest in your business are fueled by inspiration—how many by fear?

NEW-PARADIGM LEADERSHIP

The new-paradigm business environment will have new role models for leadership: the boss who drops anger in mid-tantrum to acknowledge and apologize for misdirected blame; the worker who has the courage to quit an abusive workplace to look for something better; the president of the United States, faced with the flu during a critical meeting, who finds sufficient faith and compassion to take the time he needs to nurture himself back to health rather than pushing himself to attend the meeting.

To transform America's corporate culture will require just such leaps of faith. The unrest many of us are feeling now is the early sign of a healthy spiritual awakening, the harbinger of a new era for business, an age where spiritual values are not checked at the office door.

We need to open ourselves to an expanded perspective about the meaning of true success—reminding ourselves about values that endure; trusting our own inner wisdom, our ability to take courageous action; and cradling our heads when we're tired and crabby . . . loving ourselves and having faith in life no matter what.

The challenges of the future will lead business people to call upon inner resources as never before. Those who will have the competitive advantage are the very people who have taken the time to do the difficult internal work of spiritual growth called for in this book.

The external and the internal are converging in a new paradigm that is destined to change the way we do business in this country. The irony is that by doing what seems diametrically opposed to all our culturally derived notions of what it takes to succeed, we find the only path leading to an experience of success that can endure.

You can have this experience of success in your life. This book will show you how.

THE *I CHING*: AN EXECUTIVE SUMMARY

The destinies of men are subject to immutable laws that must fulfill themselves. But man has it in his power to shape his fate, according as his behavior exposes him to the influence of benevolent or of destructive forces.

—The *I Ching*

The *I Ching* is believed to be the oldest book still in print in the world today. Over three thousand years old, the book evolved over many centuries. It is a synthesis of folk wisdom, mythology, poetry, and symbolic lessons drawn from ancient Chinese history. A book of divination as well as insight, the *I Ching* features sixty-four readings called hexagrams, each describing an archetypal life situation. Each of the sixty-four hexagrams carries with it six variations, called changing lines. By throwing three coins, the querent can arrive at a pattern of heads and tails that guides him to those readings that most accurately reflect the particular forces at play in his life at that moment in time. Unlike some other methods of divination the *I Ching* not only provides information on the forces with which the petitioner will be faced but additionally counsels the correct conduct under the circumstances. In this way he can gain the wisdom and knowledge necessary to influence positively the circumstances of his life. Paul O'Brien, who has captured the spirit of the *I Ching* in *Synchronicity,* his software version of the classic work, describes the ancient system as "an intuitive decision-making tool to help you deal with the kind of problems that logic can't handle."

At a minimum the *I Ching* has won respect as a remarkably useful tool for helping the seeker gain access to his own inner wisdom and knowledge. Seen from the point of view of "decision theory," the *I Ching* provides information that can be used either to challenge or to validate a given point of view. Taken at its most serious and profound level, the *I Ching* goes much farther, relating to the serious student as if it contains, in the words of the great psychologist Carl Jung, "a living soul."

Consulted in this spirit, the book delivers consistently intelligent and pertinent answers, sometimes complimenting, sometimes warning or scolding, always attending to the care of its student's spiritual growth—as well as providing practical, day-to-day guidance in facing life's challenges.

Jung studied the *I Ching* for thirty years, coining the word *synchronicity* to explain how and why the apparently random chance of tossing sticks (the original method) or coins could result in intelligent, targeted guidance beyond what accident alone could produce.

O'Brien explains that somehow cracking the code of synchronicity, the ancient authors of the *I Ching* managed to use the numerical laws of chance to tap into profound patterns of meaning based on the notion that how three coins happen to fall six times in a row relates to everything else impacting the seeker at that moment of time.

Whether or not you choose to develop this kind of personal relationship with the divinatory aspect of the *I Ching*, you can use its ancient words of wisdom to obtain practical guidance and knowledge that you can apply to your workplace every day of your life. For starters here are ten great notions, extrapolated from the *I Ching*'s hexagrams and changing lines, and commentary, that I have found particularly useful to me as a business executive over the years.

Ten Great Notions

NOTION NUMBER ONE: BALANCE

The *I Ching* views the world as the dynamic interplay between opposites: male and female, giving and receiving, activity and rest, rationality and faith, and so on. Every individual has opposing forces within him—as does every company. Any entity may benefit from a pure expression of either quality at any given moment. But overall, over time, it is the dynamic tension between the opposites that creates true power. This is called balance.

One of the forces that is most out of balance in Western business is the pull toward action-oriented behaviors, such as goal setting, achievement, drive, and effort, as opposed to intrinsic behaviors, such as releasing, receiving, and letting. The *I Ching* teaches that a balance of these two behaviors is more productive and beneficial in the long run than an overreliance on one at the expense of the other.

A client of our agency, a lawyer who presided over a small but busy law firm, discovered the validity of this principle in a dramatic way. As managing partner the lawyer ran the firm like it was an army. His patriarchal, authoritarian style demanded that partners and employees alike do what he say without question.

He was great at giving orders but never left space for others to provide him with input. Quite simply he did not want to receive feedback from others—which left them feeling underutilized, unheard, and unappreciated. As a result of his overemphasis on efficiency and discipline, the staff was disgruntled and disloyal, resulting in high turnover. Because of problems resulting from the chaos, he was soon forced to spend more of his time dealing with staff issues than serving his clients.

During the course of this there was one bright spot: The lawyer fell in love. He married and soon had a child. It wasn't long before he started attempting to run his family as he ran his business. His philosophy of running a family like an army began to cause so many problems with his marriage that his wife began talking about divorce. Realizing that on top of his problems at work he was losing his wife and child, our client hit bottom. It was during this period of desperation that he understood that he had been relying too exclusively on the action-oriented extreme. A friend of his, a sports psychologist, suggested that he soften his approach by integrating receptive principles into his thinking.

Rather than see business and family as a battleground, our client began to see them as playing fields. Instead of seeing business and marriage as "me versus the enemy," he began to think in terms of teamwork. He began to listen to his wife, partners, and employees, seeking their input and feedback, making room for them to express their own creativity. As he loosened his grip, staff turnover dropped dramatically. His marriage improved, and before long his practice recovered.

The *I Ching* teaches that there is a place within each of us where the forces of action and receptivity are in proper balance and one experiences true power. Keep a mental picture of cooking with a pot of water over an open fire. If the fire is too low, the water will not boil. If the fire is too hot, the water will boil away. Only when the balance of forces is just right will the water be free to do the work it was intended to do.

NOTION NUMBER TWO: CYCLES

The interplay between opposites expresses itself in a number of polarities. Those pertaining to the dynamic interplay between opposites over time are called cycles. Creativity and destruction, growth and regression, advance and retreat—these and many more contrasting and sometimes conflicting cyclical forces naturally arise in the *I Ching*'s worldview.

What is fascinating about the *I Ching*'s notion of these forces is the concept that everything is in constant movement, strengthening or weakening on a continual basis. When any particular quality gets strong enough, it eventually peaks—turning into its opposite.

The concept of cycles takes its model from nature. According to the *I Ching*, each quality contains its opposite: even in the depth of winter the roots of spring are preparing themselves to bloom again. Failure contains the roots of future success, just as in the autumn yesterday's leaves return to the earth to fertilize new growth.

Illustrating this notion is the story of Stan, a sales manager who spent the first twenty years of his career in the wine industry. After two decades the industry went into a slump, and the company Stan worked for went bankrupt. Though he was devastated by his company's failure, he assumed he would soon find a position in a wine company with a healthier financial profile. Despite his qualifications, however, he could not find a single sales-manager slot in any of the wine companies that had successfully weathered the recession.

Failure surrounded him. But after a few months of an unsuccessful job hunt, hearing the same story about pending bankruptcy everywhere he turned, Stan had a brainstorm. He realized that as a result of the failure of his company he now had experience not only in wine but also in bankruptcies and reorganization. He knew how to help other wineries learn from his experiences. He knew both the business challenges and the emotional difficulties they faced. There was indeed a demand for his services. And so Stan became a reorganization sales specialist for wine companies. With his background in sales he could work with them to maximize the opportunities they still had—as well as help them deal with the realities of reorganization. Today Stan is making a comfortable living and is excited about the meaning and results of his work.

But just as success finds its roots in failure, so does failure find its roots in success. Success is only assured on the upswing—before it reaches its peak. For the cycle of success predicts even the noblest individual's tendency to become arrogant, lose touch with his or her roots, or relax into complacency, resulting in failure—and the whole cycle begins again.

Cycles are not only internal, however. The *I Ching* sees natural cycles in corporate life—expansion and contraction and, in the economy—growth and recession. While the *I Ching* teaches us that there are some things we can do to help determine our own fates—prolonging the upswing of the cycle, for instance—the *I Ching* also offers advice on how to make the most of the down times in the cycle—without turning against ourselves or wearing ourselves out in useless resistance. There are times to push and times to be patient. Knowing what to do when is the key to getting maximum success out of any situation. When faced with a certain loss, for instance, it is possible to retreat early in the process—with one's dignity and strength preserved for an alternative approach at a later date—as opposed to waiting too long and missing one's moment.

One enterprising company has gone so far as to build their entire business around this notion. I refer to their concept as "managed failure." Operating a chain of retail party-favor stores throughout California, they jump on trends early in the process, ever-watchful for signs that the trend has peaked. Their latest triumph was the troll phenomenon—the homely plastic dolls that swept the school-age set, like Cabbage Patch Kids and Teenage Mutant Ninja Turtles before them. To capitalize on their popularity, the owner changed his stock from party favors to trolls, storing his wrapping paper and ribbons in a back room. With the change of a sign, the party-favor stores became troll stores overnight.

He continued to sell troll merchandise exclusively until he saw the first signs that the fad was dying down. As profits began to decline, he converted back to party favors store by store—anticipating the end of the trend. By the time demand declined, his troll stock was down to one shelf in each of his party-favor stores. He was then poised and ready, waiting for the next trend to hit.

NOTION NUMBER THREE: HUMILITY

In order to be alert enough to take full advantage of the natural cycles in your life, you must be humble. The *I Ching* teaches us that the "superior man" is the one who is vigilant with his own heart—free of prejudices and arrogance and open to receiving guidance from anyone at any time.

I think here of the courage of a client of ours—a salami company fighting for market share. They had received a phone call from a reporter on the staff of a major newspaper, bent on doing an exposé of food additives in salami. Their product contained nitrates—as did every other comparable salami in its category available in the mainstream marketplace. Their initial response was to ignore the call, hoping to avoid mention in the article.

When they called on us for advice, however, they were open—despite their fear—to what we had to say. We suggested that if they resisted the inquiry, they might inflame the journalist. The result could be a far larger and more damaging story than the one being planned. Rather than resist, we suggested that they cooperate fully.

They took our advice, giving up their resistance, trusting that by going with the events as they unfolded they would have the best chance of getting a fair hearing and balanced report. They decided to take on the role of educators rather than defendants. As it turned out, their nondefensive view of the role of nitrates in their part of the food industry conveyed to the reporter that there was no need for a cover-up. The article eventually took the point of view of placing the issue of additives in perspective.

Humility itself represents a polarity. The *I Ching* teaches us that exceptional modesty and conscientiousness are sure to be rewarded with success. "However, if a man is not to throw himself away, it is important that he not become empty form and subservience." Knowing who you are—and where you are at any given moment in your own personal cycle—are keys to true power.

Unlike contemporary "positive thinking" literature, the *I Ching* does not believe that if you want something badly enough and try hard enough you are assured of getting it. In *Inner Excellence* I told the story of a poet, frustrated at the rejection of her book of poems for the twentieth time, who sought out the advice of her wise aunt.

"I thought that if you courageously peel away the facade and take big risks by expressing your authentic self openly, the money will come."

Her aunt quietly poured her a glass of lemonade.

"Niece, dear," she said, "it is more likely to turn out that way when you peel down to the core and find that your authentic self contains an investment banker inside."

The *I Ching* teaches that it is critical to see yourself accurately— your strengths and your weaknesses. In some cases you might recognize that you are in a position of authority for which you are by nature really inadequate. Even in this unfortunate circumstance the *I Ching* has practical guidance for helping you rise to the occasion. In fact when humility is seen as part of the natural cycle of life, you begin to understand how, why, and when your own shortcomings can turn into your greatest virtue.

I was first taught this lesson by my father, who found himself at the beginning of his adult work life at a particularly unfortunate moment in American history: the Great Depression. My father was making a major effort to gather the tuition money for medical school. He was basically answering every ad he could get his hands on, including one particularly attractive offer to drive a truck for the Chicago Post Office.

There was just one hitch. He had no idea how to drive.

The day of the interview, applicants hoping to be selected for the precious few openings swarmed the Post Office. The interviewer strode into the room and had but one question for the throng: "Who here does not know how to drive?"

Crestfallen, my father was one of a handful who raised their hands.

"The rest of you may leave," the interviewer said. Then turning to the few whose hands had been raised, he announced, "You will start driving tomorrow."

The interviewer later explained that while it was true that he may have turned away competent drivers who had both the skills and the character for the job, by utilizing this method of selection, he could just as easily have wasted precious time with someone who had neither the character nor the skills. By this selection method he was sure of at least one thing: He was hiring honest people who had the humility and willingness to learn. Teaching them to drive was the easy part.

Being willing to see objective reality—to overcome your preferences and prejudices in order more ably to deal with what is real—is no easy task.

Illustrating this is the story of an entrepreneur I know who came from a long line of restaurateurs. For decades her family built its reputation on quality food and service. The daughter, however, decided to one-up her family's legacy. Her restaurant was going to become the new ''in spot'' in town.

Despite years of training in the importance of hiring experienced wait staff, she believed that with her eye for talent she could train anyone to serve food. But in hiring novices who carried themselves with ''attitude,'' she soon found herself overwhelmed by arrogant people who cared more about appearance and style than service.

Complaints started pouring in from customers, and turnover of wait staff was high. She was forced to admit that she did not know how to make her restaurant the next trendy spot. Humbled, she went to her family for help.

Swallowing her pride, she returned to her family's management style, an approach in keeping with her real values: to provide a place of nurturing, service, and value for her customers. She began hiring experienced wait staff—regardless of their styling. As turnover decreased and service increased, her restaurant prospered. Her business became stronger once she let go of her desire to be better than everybody else in her family. She confronted her arrogance, and business boomed.

NOTION NUMBER FOUR:
LEADERSHIP

Humility guides the "superior man" to sacrifice his own selfish aims in order to act in accordance with what he believes to be right. In times of adversity this willingness to follow the behests of a greater purpose provides "that stability which is stronger than fate."

"He who lets his spirit be broken by exhaustion certainly has no success. But if adversity only bends a man, it creates in him a power to react that is bound in time to manifest itself," says the *I Ching*.

Such an individual, exhibiting the qualities of the "superior man," will provide leadership of the highest order. Regardless of his or her title or position, or whether he or she has designated authority over others, this person will influence others by the very quality of his or her being.

Someone who discovered this notion to be true in her own career was the owner of one of the East Coast's top market-research companies. Her company was charged with the mission of providing organizations with statistics to help them make decisions concerning the launching of new products.

This woman's firm was one of the best. She had a large staff and devoted client base. Yet, as successful as she was, she found herself believing less and less in her numbers. Clients were paying enormous amounts for the surveys and calculations, passing along the costs to their customers in the form of increased prices. In her heart she realized that more often than not she had an intuitive feeling about what the answers were going to be before all concerned went to that enormous expense.

Often, she realized, her clients also had a gut feeling that was right on. More and more she saw her role as encouraging them to work through their fear and trust their own intuition—a function that ran counter to her job as owner of a numbers-based research firm. Believing that there was a better way to go about the market-research business, she began to resent the long, stressful hours spent crunching numbers. She longed to follow her heart.

Increasingly uncomfortable with the tactics her business demanded of her, she decided to sell her firm. Without knowing what was going to be next for her, she moved across the country and began to take classes in the areas of psychic development and spirituality.

She gave up her title and position in order to pursue what she felt to be in service of a greater good: a better, more honest way of approaching market research that would wean clients off of external authority and instead tune them into their own hearts for answers. Despite the financial sacrifices she was forced to make short-term, she believed that what she was doing was right for her. After a year or so she felt strong enough in her convictions to begin a consulting practice to help companies make decisions based on intuitive information rather than statistics. She was living testimony to her beliefs, attracting business to her by the very essence of her being. After two years her consulting practice was turning a profit.

The true leader is she who is willing to stand alone for what is right. Unlike the "obsequious office seeker" of the *I Ching*, who stands in opposition to the enlightened man and who throws himself at opportunities, the superior individual finds the balance between action and spontaneity on the one hand and restraint and discrimination on the other—trusting that the cycles of time will turn in her favor sooner or later.

NOTION NUMBER FIVE: CORRECT RELATIONSHIP

Not everyone is a born leader. Though we may all be equal in our potential for willingness to serve the common good, we are not all equal in our abilities and levels of courage. But unlike Western culture, with its emphasis on individual achievement, the *I Ching* sees nobility in serving superiors joyfully. If you recognize that you do not have the requisite stability to stand alone for what is right as the focal point for your community, the *I Ching* urges you to lend your support to someone who does, to join with others of like mind who are being led by someone who is worthy of your support.

In exchange for your devoted service the *I Ching* teaches the leader "not to abuse his great influence" but rather to use it for the good of all. "An enlightened ruler and an obedient servant—this is the condition on which great progress depends."

I witnessed this notion in action during my exchange with Tom, a reporter from a metropolitan newspaper. New on the job, Tom was to write a story for a business column on *Inner Excellence*. He had been charged with translating my principles into a "how-to"-formatted column—a challenge beyond his expertise, since the principles do not stem from the traditional business concepts with which he was familiar.

Being new in his position, Tom wanted to prove his ability as a self-starter. Yet, after sitting with the material for much of the day, he realized that he was lost. Humbly, he went to his editor and asked for help. As Tom reported to me after his column appeared, the editor had been delighted. More often young reporters failed to ask for help early enough in the process, wasting precious time and turning in unacceptable material. By asking for help early on he had demonstrated correct relationship by willingly taking on the subservient role in a mentor relationship with his editor, which resulted in many plum assignments.

The editor, too, illustrated the principle of correct relationship by having created the kind of environment where even the weakest member of the team could admit shortcomings without fear of retribution. The editor and newspaper benefited from such an open and accepting culture, inhabited by inspired individuals who, freed from the burden of illusion, use their precious time and energy to create rather than to protect.

In further support of this notion, I recall the story of an interior decorator in a small community who attempted to build a practice on her own. The bane of her life was a competitor who had a years-long lead on her as well as an innate sense of marketing.

After several years struggling to establish herself, the disadvantaged decorator finally took up the suggestion of one of her friends. Overcoming her pride, she went to the competitor and asked if she could fold her handful of clients into the larger company. Not only was the competitor willing, she was delighted to take her on—and not as an employee but as an associate.

Business boomed for both of them as, through their combined forces, they became for all intents and purposes the only game in town.

NOTION NUMBER SIX: GOODNESS

You have been given a true nature that is innately good. By surrendering to the divine spirit within you, you will instinctively be led to do what is right and best under any given circumstance, regardless of how it may appear to you or others at the time. It is through surrender to who and what you really are—the expression of the fullest development of your nature—that you will achieve the supreme experience of success. Your personal Tao beckons you to follow what is good in yourself courageously and patiently, both mirroring and expressing the great Tao, the ultimate expression of regeneration, life, light, and goodness in the universe.

The truth of this principle can be seen in the story of Sybil, a friend who is passionate about the subject of child abuse. Eventually her expertise and credibility in the field built to the point that she was asked to undertake speaking engagements on the subject. This terrified her.

To assuage her fear, Sybil began to seek out the top speakers in her city, attending their lectures and seminars, studying their style and technique. Eventually, when she felt she understood what it took to keep the attention of an audience, she took to the podium.

Beginning her talks with a joke, Sybil brought a snappy, lighthearted approach to her delivery. She wanted her audiences to like her and give her positive reviews. She was shocked and dismayed therefore when she got nearly universal negative feedback. Seeking out the advice of her peers, Sybil realized that she had put pleasing and entertaining her audiences before her true purpose in taking to the stage—educating and alarming her audiences about the horrors of child abuse.

She decided to stop worrying about her performance and concentrate on her real feelings about the material. In essence she surrendered to the divine spirit within her, leading her to expose her true feelings and purpose. Sybil became a controversial speaker, even abrasive at times. Rather than receiving the universal acclaim she'd sought so hard to achieve, she polarized audiences. Some agreed with her. Some opposed her. But the difficult issues Sybil addressed were at last being dealt with honestly and effectively.

Sybil surrendered to her true nature, giving expression to the greater good. The more she gave up the goal of being well liked, and instead took the more courageous path of devoting herself to being true to herself, the more in demand as a speaker Sybil became.

Another example of this principle in action is the story of Thomas, an urban planner who had been raised to uphold the family tradition of professional work. In devoting himself to his career Thomas soon realized that he had little passion for urban development. The career was not a total washout, however, as he enjoyed the aspects of urban planning that had to do with landscaping. In fact he realized that his real love was gardening itself—working with the soil and planting organically. Following his heart, Thomas left his prestigious job. He moved from his suburban ranch house and took a shack that came with a plot of land and began organic gardening. His passion soon blossomed into a success far greater than any he could have ever achieved as an urban planner. Thomas founded what became one of the most respected nonprofit organic-seed companies in the country.

This kind of success cannot come about by pushing or manipulating for personal advantage or reward. It will not come to you when you try to take a shortcut, allowing the quest for personal glory and separation from the common good to fuel your actions. The *I Ching* tells us that the way to progress toward supreme success is simply this: "When he discovers good in others, he should imitate it and thus make everything on earth his own. If he perceives something bad in himself, let him rid himself of it . . . This ethical change represents the most important increase of personality."

NOTION NUMBER SEVEN: PERSEVERANCE

Grow slow and send your roots deep. The *I Ching* teaches that the good things that happen to you come as a result of the work that you do on your character:

A man brings about real increase by producing in himself the conditions for it, that is, through receptivity to and love of the good. Thus the thing for which he strives comes of itself, with the inevitability of natural law. Where increase is thus in harmony with the highest laws of the universe, it cannot be prevented by any constellation of accidents. . . .

For such a man perseverance over time is the key factor determining success. You pile up many small things along the way in order to discover eventually that you have achieved something great. The *I Ching* uses water as its image for perseverance, which sets an example for right conduct by flowing effortlessly around the shoals of life's challenges. When water meets an obstacle, it piles up on itself, eventually overflowing the top to freedom.

Such a notion was at work not long ago when my agency went after a new client. We really wanted this particular client, investing a lot of time and energy researching his industry, putting together a great proposal. The industry this client represented is highly competitive and specialized. We were eager to get a toehold in the field—and this client presented the perfect breakthrough for us.

The presentation went well, and we thought we had won the account. But before long a too-thin envelope arrived, letting us know the bad news: Another agency had been selected.

We were miserable—but our upset proved to be temporary. For before long a second company in that industry heard that their competitor had hired a P. R. firm. They came to us and asked us to handle their account—at a bigger retainer than we had proposed to our original contact. All of the work we had done to get into the industry in the first place, although it had seemed wasted, actually qualified us for the quick start-up this company was seeking. Had we won the first account, we would never have been tapped for this better piece of business.

NOTION NUMBER EIGHT:
CONDITIONS

In a culture that values the illusion that "you can have it all," it's both sobering and liberating to learn from the *I Ching* that "human life on earth is conditioned and unfree." The root may choose to blossom in winter—but it is not free to do so. There are harmonious and beneficent forces of the cosmos that operate in our lives. We find our greatest success when we surrender our arrogant efforts to control and dominate our lives for personal gain—and allow ourselves to act in concert with these forces.

A business associate in my circle of friends, the personnel director of a big insurance company, learned about this notion firsthand. A dedicated careerwoman, she believed that if you want to get the job done right, you have to do it yourself. She truly believed that if she was not there, the company would fall apart. She worked nights, weekends—easily eighty hours a week.

Then she became pregnant. She thought she could surpass any challenge fate brought to her, but this was a problem pregnancy that required bed rest. Suddenly she had to back off from her responsibilities and do only the essential parts that could be done at home on her laptop computer in bed.

She was forced to trust that her staff would rise to the occasion. The staff, who had been sorely underutilized throughout her reign, gladly assumed the responsibility, and all the work was accomplished at the same high level of quality. In fact the staff became more effective and efficient as a result. Morale was at an all-time high.

After the baby was born, the personnel director returned to work. She resisted the old habit of resuming her prepregnancy workathon. Through enforced limitation she had learned that she was not a one-man band but part of a team. By embracing this notion, she cut her work week by fifty percent—and watched productivity soar.

71

Another example of someone coming to term with life's conditions is that of Clark, a multitalented man who has followed two streams throughout his career—as singer and as motivational speaker. Unwilling to choose between the two, and believing that he could have it all, Clark split his time between the two disparate worlds, achieving moderate success in each. As he approached forty, he felt opportunities to make it really big as a singer in an increasingly youth-dominated market slipping away. He realized that he could choose to fight the stereotypes—or he could flow with the conditions time and fate were imposing upon him. Clark made the decision to keep singing as his hobby—to volunteer his time to perform for hospitals and in nursing homes—but to concentrate his energies on motivational speaking. This was just the boost his speaking needed. Clark's career as a lecturer and trainer in the field of motivational speaking took off, as did his own experience of success and fulfillment. Life's limitations had opened its great black cloak to reveal wonderful gifts—opportunities for happiness beyond his wildest dreams—inside.

The *I Ching* teaches that "unlimited possibilities are not suited to man; if they existed, his life would only dissolve in the boundless. To become strong, a man's life needs the limitations ordained by duty and voluntarily accepted. The individual attains significance as a free spirit only by surrounding himself with these limitations and by determining for himself what his duty is."

The plant world owes its life to the fact that it clings to the soil in which the forces of life express themselves. It is the same in the life of man. In order to "attain influence on earth," you must surrender to your true nature.

However, this does not mean that if you do so, everything will subsequently go your way. The *I Ching* teaches us to appreciate that even opposition has its purpose. When you surrender to your human limitations, there is only one way left to find fulfillment: by cultivating an appreciation for the full cycle of creativity and destruction that life contains. When you surrender to life, you experience everything from ecstasy to despair. The cycle of life will bring you opportunities to celebrate—and to grieve. You submit to uncertainty and unconsciousness. The *I Ching* teaches that the key to having a quiet heart is to give up resistance and accept where you are right now, no matter how uncomfortable that place may be.

NOTION NUMBER NINE:
SIMPLICITY

The *I Ching* has no difficulty with the concepts of prosperity and "supreme success," but warns that accumulation of wealth at the top will cause the entire structure to fall. Rather than pile up riches for one's personal use, the *I Ching* suggests that the reader consider the concept of defining for oneself what is enough. Extolling the virtues of self-imposed limitation, the *I Ching* advises that "if we live economically in normal times, we are prepared for times of want."

In keeping with contemporary environmental thinking, the *I Ching* teaches that the world has limited resources and that voluntary simplicity is one way to live harmoniously with cosmic forces. But even moderation needs moderation. "If a man should seek to impose galling limitations upon his own nature, it would be injurious. And if he should go too far imposing limitations on others, they would rebel." The *I Ching* guides us to find and define for ourselves the "middle path."

One businessman who has successfully walked the middle path was a promoter of environmental expositions. Gene Farb, who was an early client of ours, felt passionate about raising the awareness level of individuals concerning environmental issues.

To foster an environmental ethic in the population at large, he, along with several partners came up with the idea of organizing expositions that would travel to cities across the country every year. Held in large arenas, the shows would educate attendees on environmental issues and would feature booths of related products and services. Unfortunately, although the shows were well organized and attended, the investment in both time and money to produce the venture was enormous. After a number of rounds Gene and his partners called it quits.

There was one bright spot, however. A booth Gene ran with the assistance of his family within each expo had generated a lot of interest and sales. The booth had both demonstrated and sold products related to conserving water, using solar energy, reducing smoke emissions from fireplaces, and so on.

Gene realized that he did not need the elaborate large-scale expo to make his point. A small storefront retail operation would do the trick. Going the simplest route possible, he and his partners put their money into presenting these products at the best price possible—avoiding advertising hype and fancy store displays. The store was called the Whole Earth Access Company.

The store was so well received that it has now grown organically into a number of department-size locations in northern California. Part of the appeal is the simple, warehouse feel to shelving and lighting—the lack of hype and the emphasis on education. It was the middle path for Gene and his partners that proved to be the most direct route to their greatest success.

Another company benefiting from the middle path is Patagonia, a manufacturer and retailer of outdoor clothing and equipment. Through the eighties the company grew to be one of the country's most influential mail-order retailers, fueled largely by their desire to make as much money as possible to donate to the environmental movement. By fall of 1991 the company offered 420 styles in their catalog, ninety more than the previous year.

Recognizing the irony that by "growth for growth's sake" they were inadvertently contributing to pollution (i.e., cotton used in clothing requires the use of pesticides that over time make soil infertile) they made the radical decision to simplify. "We are limiting Patagonia's growth in the United States with the eventual goal of halting growth altogether," they announced in their catalog.

The company subsequently dropped 30 percent of its clothing line, commenting, "What does this mean to you? Well, last fall you had a choice of five ski pants; now you may choose between two. This is, of course, un-American, but two styles of ski pants are all anyone needs."

What has simplifying meant to Patagonia? Ironically, 1992 was Patagonia's most profitable year to date.

NOTION NUMBER TEN: VIGILANCE

The *I Ching* asks you to remain ever-vigilant in order to recognize those moments that contain the seeds of the future—success or failure—for you. The *I Ching* teaches that indifference to detail is "the root of all evil": "Here we have the rule indicating the usual course of history. But this rule is not inescapable law. He who understands it is in position to avoid its effects by dint of unremitting perseverance and caution."

The most important prerequisite for success is to become ever more aware of shifts in the cycles of time so that you may make whatever corrections are called for in order to stay in harmony with the forces of the cosmos. You can do this only if you have sufficient humility to let go of your relentless pursuit of personal aims, surrender to your innate nature, and devote yourself to the common good. If this calls forth from you the necessity and the willingness to stand alone, you will find the only expression of true leadership that can survive the vicissitudes of fate.

Such was the case of Steven, a sales representative for a large moving company. The culture of his company called for exaggerated claims about how their movers could outperform the competition. As the inevitable complaints and problems arose, Steven felt worse and worse about his company's culture. Finally he decided that he could no longer misrepresent himself to his customers. Recognizing the seeds of the future—that only failure and unhappiness lay on the road ahead should he persist in working against his own spirit—he began to look for another job.

Throughout his job search Steven remained vigilant, not getting swept up in offers or cultures that dazzled on the surface but left him with a funny feeling in the pit of his stomach. His wife worried as the bank account diminished, urging Steven to "get off his high horse" and take the next position, regardless of his doubts. But Steven

75

held firm. Before too long, he bumped into an old college friend who told him about a small, off-beat moving company they had used on their last move. The company sounded perfect to Steven. He called and discovered that they were searching for someone with his credentials and background to join their team. Steven joined forces with the firm, delighted that his new group shared his growing awareness of honesty being the best policy.

Instead of presenting customers with a canned sales pitch, he found himself able to tell them the whole truth—educating them about the risks involved with moving household goods from one place to another. Having put forth his disclaimer, he then assured his customers that he would do everything humanly possible to minimize damage. He was sincere, authentic—and this attitude created a level of trust with his customers that proved to be more effective than his previous attempts at getting new business.

Given the nature of life's cycles, at any given time aspects of yourself are growing while others are dying. The *I Ching* teaches you that all that matters is to carry out all that has to be done—thoroughness—and going forward. Take time to grieve that which you are leaving behind, but invest your life energy in that which is birthing. This is the way to supreme success.

These, then, are Ten Great Notions extracted from the *I Ching* that I have found to be particularly useful in today's workplace. They are, in fact, philosophical underpinnings of what we are calling ''The New Paradigm.'' How ironic it is that the ''new'' paradigm shares so much in common with the wisdom of three thousand years ago. As the *I Ching* instructs us about cycles of time, so has the advice contained in its poetic images—so vital and pertinent three thousand years ago—cycled back into our consciousness renewed and revitalized.

How grateful I am to have found such a wise teacher, able to transcend the trappings of one historical era or another, to provide advice for handling business problems today. In the next section of this book, gently guided by my many hours immersed in its perspective, I will respond to one hundred tough business challenges, leading you to resolution whenever possible—and to invocations for hope and recovery when practical approaches to problem solving fall short.

Prepare to be surprised.

ONE HUNDRED TOUGH BUSINESS PROBLEMS

What is born of heaven feels related to what is above. What is born of earth feels related to what is below. Each follows its kind.

—Confucius

AUTHOR'S NOTE

It was easy for me to identify one hundred tough business problems that the contemporary worker is likely to face in the course of his or her career. Many of these were taken from the question-and-answer sessions I eagerly anticipate at the conclusion of each of my speeches, and from letters to the editor of my publication *Inner Excellence: The Bulletin of Success and Spirituality*, Others were extracted from the thousands of tough business problems I myself have faced during the course of my two decades in business. In fact I would modestly proclaim that if I excel at anything, it is at stumbling across tough business issues.

If you have a pressing question or concern, you can scan the problems and see if one or several in particular resonate to the issue. Feel free to turn directly to those specific problems and responses. You could also use this book as a simple divinatory tool by opening randomly to any page and read for meaning wherever your eyes happen to fall.

To get maximum value out of this book, however, I suggest that you take the time to read through all of the problems and their responses sequentially. Some problems that may not at first seem pertinent may contain wisdom and knowledge applicable to your specific set of circumstances after all. But even more importantly, by reading through all of the responses, you will begin to train yourself to a new way of thinking and being in the workplace. You will begin to see your life, and the lives of those with whom you work, differently.

In the body of my responses, when I credit or quote the *I Ching*, I am referring to either the translation of the ancient text or commentary on it, by Confucius and others, as shared specifically in the Wilhelm/ Baynes edition. Additionally, quotes by Confucius are from Lin Yutang's *The Wisdom of Confucius* or *The Analects of Confucius*, translated by Lionel Giles.

As you begin to apply this new way of being in the workplace, remember that your ultimate task is to stay in close communication with your own inner wisdom. No person, no book, no belief system, no technique should ever come between you and your own common sense.

Are you ready?

Good. We begin with problem number one: How would Confucius ask for a raise?

1

Managing Your Career

If a man goes on quietly and perseveringly working at the removal of resistances, success comes in the end.

—The *I Ching*

TOUGH BUSINESS PROBLEM #1

How would Confucius ask for a raise?

The *I Ching* teaches us that "the superior man acquaints himself with many sayings of antiquity in order to strengthen his character"— and, while he's at it, quite possibly to rake in a higher salary.

Fortunately you have access to the guidance of the *I Ching*, the very book that Confucius consulted when faced with challenges in his life. From this you can deduce how Confucius would have approached the sticky problem of asking for a raise, and can profit from that example.

Let's start with some good news: You want something from somebody that you are afraid they might not want to give you.

That's good news? It is if you think like Confucius. Because in this situation the *I Ching* teaches you to recognize and welcome the dynamic tension inherent in opposition. Opposition, when seen as a positive rather than a threatening state, leads naturally to the imperative to bridge it. It is, in fact, the source of all innovation and creativity.

Seen this way, the question becomes: How can you make opposition work for you?

Step One: Most bosses like to think giving you a raise is their idea. Even when you're facing the most receptive of conditions, it will take some time to implant and reinforce the notion with sufficient subtlety that you deserve the raise. Therefore begin by initiating what we will call here your "salary-increase cycle" a season or two *before* you plan on getting your next raise. If you try to speed up the timetable, you may find yourself like a farmer running after his runaway horse— the more you chase it, the faster and farther it will run. But if you back off, eventually it will come to you of its own accord.

This does not mean you sit back passively and wait for your next review to roll around. Instead initiate your salary-increase cycle now by researching your company's salary-review policies. Does your company have a mechanism in place for salary reviews? Do reviews take place annually? Every six months? Perhaps you are overdue and getting your raise will be as simple as reminding your boss that you are due for a salary review.

He or she may say, "You're right. You've done a great job this year. Here's the money you want, a great job title, a corner office, and a BMW." (Miracles do happen. Remember always to let yourself be prepared to welcome them.)

Step Two: But if you are not overdue for a review—and/or your miracle fails to arrive—you can take an active role in initiating your salary-increase cycle by asking your boss for a nonsalary review.

At a nonsalary review you ask for an assessment of your current performance. You are not doing this in order to feel bad about or defend what you have or haven't done. Rather you are on a fact-finding mission to ascertain your starting position; in order to get to where you're going, you've got to figure out where you are now.

Don't wait. Do it as soon as you can. And listen with an open mind to the information you are receiving.

Step Three: Step Three is to then make your boss a member of your salary-increase committee. You are the other member. You do this by thanking your boss for his or her feedback and then asking for help in setting a salary goal based on performance criteria you will meet by your next salary-review date. Make sure you both know when that date will be—and what your expectations will be for that important meeting.

In order to facilitate your boss's scheduling an acceptable salary increase for you, you should have a salary-increase range in mind— a low end (the least you would expect to receive) and a high end (the number you would be thrilled to get). Then place your energy and expectations in the middle—somewhere between the two but on the gutsier end of comfortable.

Let the salary you decide upon for yourself be inspiring to you without being intimidating. It should be a number that not only reflects your contribution to the company to date, but is big enough to accommodate the growing you intend to do between this and your next review.

If your boss "helps" you set a salary goal that is on track with your middle-range raise—great. If it's on the high end—greater. If, however, it's on the low end, your nonsalary review is the time to plant the seed for higher expectations. You simply say, "I think I can easily achieve those goals to warrant the salary raise you're talking about. But what more would I need to accomplish between now and then if I were to set my goals for something higher? . . . What I have in mind is . . ."

Step Four: Once your boss has bought into your plan, it is up to you to keep him or her informed of your progress toward your goal. Immediately after the nonsalary-review meeting, send a thank-you note, gently repeating the salary increase you have mutually set as your goal—and what you've agreed your course of action should be.

The occasional memo and informal report recounting your successes toward that goal will be sufficient to keep the ball in play.

Step Five: By the time your agreed-upon review date rolls around, your boss will be more than likely to present you with your raise— proud of how brilliantly he or she managed your growth in the company.

You will have obtained this positive result by acting in harmony with the demands of the time.

Confucius says that the superior man "composes his mind before he speaks; he makes his relations firm before he asks for something." By attending to these matters, "the superior man gains complete security. But if a man is brusque in his movements, others will not cooperate. If he is agitated in his words, they awaken no echo in others. If he asks for something without having first established relations, it will not be given to him."

So, in summary, how would Confucius ask for a raise?

The answer: He would simply *become* the person who makes a higher salary.

If you've brought your best to the situation and don't get the raise you'd like, see Tough Business Problem #55.

If you get the raise but instead of feeling elated, feel strangely depressed, see Tough Business Problem #21.

TOUGH BUSINESS PROBLEM #2

I've just been handed a great opportunity! I love my job— and now I've been offered a promotion into a bigger position. Why am I upset?

While others are busy shaking your hand, I'd like to offer my heart-felt support for your greatest accomplishment: your willingness to acknowledge your true feelings on the matter. Many of us get so swept up in the excitement of new opportunities that we forget to ask ourselves what it is we really want.

When fate comes to you bearing such apparently lovely gifts, it is easy to be seduced into giving up your most precious freedom: the right to set your own goals. Remember, you have the right to set goals that inspire excitement rather than upset. You have the right to fulfill your destiny at a pace supportive of all aspects of yourself—physical, spiritual, intellectual, and emotional. It is up to you to determine how far and how fast you want to progress—and, more importantly, how you define progress in the first place. Remember, you do have a choice.

Given all the applause you hear when you walk down the office corridor, it may be tempting to dismiss your upset as the normal jitters that one would expect to feel when taking on a new challenge. And you could be right.

But a wise friend once advised me that when faced with a choice such as the one that confronts you, there's always one sure way to make the best decision: "Go with the growth."

But where is the growth in this for you?

Is it to push through your fear and take on the new position? Or could it be something quite new and different for you?

Let's stop to consider for a moment how rare and wonderful it is that you have found something you love to do. Although everyone is tugging at your sleeve urging you forward, you know that it is the stability of your current position that is allowing you to grow in new and different ways in your life. Perhaps the confidence you feel in this job is giving you the courage to experiment with new ways of working—pacing, for instance, or creative interactions with subordinates. You have been singled out for promotion for the very qualities that could be relegated to the back burner if you were to be given new and different responsibilities at this time. At the same time there may be elements of the new job that don't appeal to you. Perhaps there's more travel involved. Or longer hours.

In fact when you allow yourself to explore your feelings and motives fully, you may recognize that your urge to accept is fueled primarily by ego and greed.

Perhaps while the whole company whispers that you are blowing this great opportunity because you're scared, you are, in fact standing firm with the greatest degree of courage you've ever had to call forth from yourself in your life.

Only you know where the edge of growth is for you.

If you would like to take the position but are afraid of making the wrong choice, see Tough Business Problem #49.

If you would like to pass on the position but feel you are obligated to take it, see Tough Business Problem #90.

TOUGH BUSINESS PROBLEM #3

I like my job for now, but I can't imagine doing this the rest of my life. How long do I wait before I start working on a long-term career I will want to stick with?

The *I Ching* teaches that when a spring first gushes forth, it does not know where it will go. It bounds forward rushing past boulders and trees until it meets the first deep place along its path. It tarries on that spot for as long as it takes, filling up the place that appears to be blocking its progress. Nothing can trap the water for very long or alter its nature. When the time is right, the level rises above the bank and spills over to proceed on its way.

The lesson the spring contains for you is that you are already working on your long-term career.

Have faith that you can trust your own happiness. This is the first deep place along your way. As your level rises toward the top, have faith that you will see the empty riverbed beyond, beckoning to you. You will know where and when to go next. You will not have to make an effort at this—nor drive yourself to fulfillment. Rather, when your moment has come, you will tumble over the edge joyfully and will effortlessly proceed onward.

Have faith that you possess the skills to deal with whatever will come up for you along the way. If you feel stalled or stuck, you can simply flow around the obstacles.

You would prefer to have control over your progress, your timing, your future. Then know this: that you have the right to have faith every moment of your journey, during the depressions as well as the advances. Have faith—this much you can control. But give up the rest. To control your course more than this will be to limit your adventure.

If you feel you are not fulfilling your potential, see Tough Business Problem #13.

If you like what you're doing but your family or friends are pressuring you to leave this job, see Tough Business Problem #42.

TOUGH BUSINESS PROBLEM #4

I've had a terrific relationship with my boss, but now it's time to move on. I've got a job offer I'd like to accept, but I don't know how to handle this without hurting his feelings.

Your desire to spare your boss's feelings is thoughtful—but also shortsighted. Even if it's painful for both of you at the moment, you can honor and serve the integrity of your relationship only when each player in a relationship is being true to himself or herself.

You serve no one, not your boss and certainly not yourself, when you deny your inner imperative out of a sense of false loyalty—the honorable but misguided effort to avoid the pain and discomfort of growth for all of the parties involved. Relationships lose their vitality; inspiration is replaced by duty; exhaustion and burnout slip in through the cracks of self-denial. Even with the best of intentions, when you squash your imperative to grow for the sake of another, you become an energy drain to the very organization you are trying to protect and preserve.

If you truly care about your boss and his company, then you best serve his needs by being willing to recognize and act on that moment in your life when it is time to move on.

To the degree that you can truly adopt this enlightened point of view, you will handle the separation with grace and style. It is fear that keeps you guarding your departure like an ugly secret, leaking or springing it out indelicately when your boss is least expecting it. You second-guess yourself on the best time and place. You manipulate and strategize. When you finally do spit it out, your news comes veiled in half-truths, excuses, accusations, or apologies. None of these are appropriate.

The way to handle this situation is to let your boss in on your thought process as soon as it becomes clear to you that you are feeling the imperative to leave. Yes—even before you have begun your job search, before you've launched your networking process.

But, you say, if I tell my boss about it, won't he fire me or let me go?

You said you have a terrific relationship with your boss. Doesn't that mean you've respected each other? Valued each other's honesty? Encouraged each other to take risks? If that's true, then you should be true to the spirit of that relationship by bringing truth and honesty to the end, just as you did to the beginning and middle.

The disciple Tsekung asked Confucius, "Is there one single word that can serve as a principle of conduct for life?"

Confucius replied, "Perhaps the word *reciprocity* will do. Do not do unto others what you do not want others to do unto you."

If you have the courage to let your boss in on your process, you may well be pleasantly surprised. Perhaps he has been expecting it for some time. Perhaps he has ideas or contacts for you to help you along.

Purposes diverge. Healthy players in the business arena recognize this as the bittersweet nature of relationship. Rather than resist the possibility of change, transition, and ultimately separation in their work lives, they hold their working relationships lovingly but lightly. You thought you were relating to each other and that the joy of your partnership derived from that connection. But the truth is that before you connected with each other, each of you first had to establish a relationship with your own inner purposes. The degree to which your purposes coincided is the degree to which your relationship succeeded.

Your attention is best placed not in loyalty to the other individual but rather in the dictates of your own heart. The enlightened boss knows that it is in his own best self-interest to encourage his subordinates to follow their inner convictions—even if that same voice that has had him serving the company so well over the years is the one that is now taking that great employee away. The experienced boss has faith that out of his ability to hold a trusting relationship to you has come an elevated ability to hold an even more trusting relationship with the next employee. He has learned the key to empowering individuals. While he may well miss the particular character and flavor you brought to the workplace, your departure brings him, too, to the portal of his next stage of development as a manager.

Not that this kind of change feels good, for either of you. We want our transitions to be easy and painless. But the truth is, following your convictions often demands a sacrifice. On the most superficial level you will sacrifice the comfort of day-to-day interactions with someone you can count on. You may well feel regret over this loss. At a deeper level, you may have to sacrifice the idea that you are a person who doesn't cause others pain. But even more pertinently, in this case you may have to sacrifice the notion you hold about yourself that you know what's best for your boss . . . what he really wants or needs.

The truth is that all you can know for certain in this situation is that you have a clear indication—from both internal and external sources—that for you to be true to yourself, you must move on.

Do you trust this voice? If so, you will be able to take a leap of faith to a new perspective: that if you follow the dictates of your heart, the results will be the best possible for all concerned.

If you honor your long-term relationship, letting your boss in on your process early on, and you get fired before you've got another job lined up, see Tough Business Problem #58.

TOUGH BUSINESS PROBLEM #5

I was the best qualified for the promotion—but the offer went to somebody else. Should I fight it?

Often, life's challenges come to you like a tangled ball of string. You know there's a place in there for you to begin—but where is it? How will you ever find the right thing to do? You may have to pick the issue apart strand by strand in order to gain the insight you seek. Here's an exercise that I call "Dialogue with Your Higher Self." Use it to work out this—or any Tough Business Problem—and you will find that you've had the answer inside yourself all along.

DIALOGUE WITH YOUR HIGHER SELF

What situation in your life are you most eager to resolve right now?
What outcome would you most like to achieve?
How have you tried to resolve this situation so far?
What was it about this approach that did not work?
How do you feel about this situation?
What judgments have you made about this situation—or about the role you have played in it to date?
What payoff or benefit have you received from having this situation in your life?
What other way could you get the same payoff that would be better for you?
What is the truth about this situation?
What must you accept about this situation?
What can you change about this situation?
What would you like to see happen?

How would you be impacted if this situation were resolved?
What one thing are you willing to change to obtain the resolution you
would like?

Now that you've become acquainted with the "Dialogue" process,
let's take a test run on this useful track. Whatever your particular set
of circumstances, the "Dialogue" is guaranteed to give you the benefit of an expanded perspective.

A SAMPLE DIALOGUE

What situation in your life are you most eager to resolve right now?
I don't have the promotion I deserved to get.

What outcome would you most like to achieve?
I want the job I deserve.

How have you tried to resolve this situation so far?
Talked to my friends in and out of the company about it.

What was it about this approach that did not work?
They don't have the power to get me the promotion.

How do you feel about this situation?
I feel mad and upset.

What judgments have you made about this situation—or about the
role you have played in it to date?
*I hate my boss—she lets people kiss up to her and gets influenced by
the sizzle, throwing the steak in the trash. I'm sick of letting myself
get thrown in the trash.*

What payoff or benefit have you received from having this situation
in your life?
I knew this about my boss for a long time, but I didn't want to bring

push to shove because I wanted to stay in the position long enough that no one could accuse me of being a jobhopper. I'm ambitious and my résumé is important to me.

What other way could you get the same payoff that would be better for you?
I hadn't stopped to realize that I've already stayed long enough to build an impressive-enough résumé. No one will accuse me of being a jobhopper.

What is the truth about this situation?
I've been in this position long enough. It's no fun working for somebody I don't respect, even if I do like the company. I didn't jockey for the promotion because I don't really want to keep working for my boss. That's why I haven't fought it yet either. The last thing I want to do is get trapped in a position of greater responsibility that has to report to someone like her. I feel better now that I can admit that staying in the job as long as I did and refraining from fighting for the promotion was an unconscious career strategy—not a lack of respect for myself.

What must you accept about this situation?
I'd love my boss to be different—but I've already tried everything I know how to do to change her. I give up. If I go directly to her superior, it will be bad for me politically. I guess, truth be told, I've already gotten everything I can hope to get out of this situation. While I'd love to stay with the company, if I want to go for what I deserve, I must accept that I've got to be willing to leave.

What can you change about this situation?
I can begin looking for another job. I can use my friends in the company so that word slips into the corporate grapevine and will quite possibly reach the ears of my boss's superiors.

What would you like to see happen?
I would like to line up another job, let my boss know, and then have her and her superiors beg me to stay—maybe even come up with a

competitive offer within this company that's better than the promotion I missed out on—but reporting to someone I respect.

How would you be impacted if this situation were resolved?
Either way I'll be better off than I was before this fiasco.

What one thing are you willing to change to obtain the resolution you would like?
I am willing to start the gossip ball rolling, telling my friends in the company that I am starting to look for a new position.

By the way, this sample dialogue was based on a real story that happened to a friend of mine—an executive in the clothing business. And what was the outcome?

Sandy played her cards well. When top management got wind of her dissatisfaction, they miraculously found a position for her in the company. It wasn't just any position, by the way—it was her former boss's job.

She won't be needing her résumé for quite some time.

If on top of everything else the job went to somebody with flawed integrity, see Tough Business Problem #63.

If the real reason you want to fight for the job is because you hate to lose, see Tough Business Problem #89.

If getting passed by served as a wake-up call and, like it or not, you now realize you are in transition either to a new relationship to your job—or to a new job entirely, see Tough Business Problem #58.

TOUGH BUSINESS PROBLEM #6

The job interview went swimmingly, but it's been several weeks and they haven't called me back. They've asked not to be called. How do I stay on top of this without turning them off by bugging them too much?

Take comfort from the fact that you presented yourself so well when you had the opportunity and that, as far as you could tell, you were well received. Although it might be a reach for you in this moment of anxious anticipation, the truth is your ability to connect with yourself and others in the stress-laden context of a job interview is truly more important to you in the long run than whether or not you land this particular position.

So many things can come up on their end that are beyond your control: They lose a major client and the job disappears; they decide to promote from in-house; the boss's husband decides to come back out of retirement to take this position—you name it. It is not a reflection on you. The first thing is to separate out the potential outcome, whatever it may be, from your experience of who you are and what you deserve. While you are waiting for their response, rest assured that you are destined to land the job of your dreams. Perhaps it will be this one—perhaps one even better is waiting for its moment to arrive. You are getting ripe. Soon you will be picked. Which will be the lucky company that gets you?

In this positive frame of mind you will be able to make the best decisions concerning how and when to follow up. For instance they asked not to be called—but they said nothing of writing. A letter following the interview thanking them for their time, reiterating your desire to work for the company, and outlining briefly why you think it's such a good match is one small gesture that can set you apart from the competition. As the days unfold, continue to look for opportunities to be in communication. You see a news item about the competition that might be of interest to your interviewer? Pass it along. You have a brainstorm about how one of their products might be positioned in the marketplace? Send it. Eventually, when you think that they've had sufficient time to make a decision, go ahead and call. You have the right not to be left hanging indefinitely. If they really want you, your making the call won't change their minds.

Whatever the outcome turns out to be, the key is not to become overly invested in this opportunity as the only job for you. In fact the best thing for you to do while waiting to hear back from them is to continue your job search with renewed enthusiasm.

The *I Ching* teaches that if a man cultivates within himself qualities of character—such as strength, faith, and perseverance—he will not have to force offers to come to him. Those that are meant for him will come of their own free will. "When the quiet power of a man's own character is at work, the effects produced are right. All those who are receptive to the vibrations of such a spirit will then be influenced."

If this offer doesn't come through and there's no other job that could possibly lend your life meaning, see Tough Business Problem #59.

If you get depressed and fear that your negative attitude spells doom, see Tough Business Problem #88.

TOUGH BUSINESS PROBLEM #7

I just graduated from college Phi Beta Kappa, and all I can find in the industry of my choice are secretarial jobs. Should I live at home and continue to hold out for something better, or should I grab what's available?

The secret to success is simple: You can start anywhere. The important thing is to make your beginning. Where and how should you start? Start the only place you can: exactly where you are right now. And where is that? In a situation where only secretarial jobs are available.

Take the secretarial job. As you act, you put forces in motion that will bring to you new opportunities. The sooner you begin, the sooner new possibilities will open up for you.

If you take the job and hate it, see Tough Business Problem #44.

If you feel that by taking this job you are not living up to your potential, see Tough Business Problem #13.

If you take the job and feel that you really ought to be doing your boss's job, see Tough Business Problem #11.

TOUGH BUSINESS PROBLEM #8

I've just landed my first job, and I've already made a mess of things. I'm trying hard to please my boss by doing what I think he wants—and then the whole thing blows up in my face. What's wrong with me?

The *I Ching* teaches, "In the time of youth, folly is not an evil. One may succeed in spite of it." In other words the great gift of being young is that it is the only time in your life when you have a good excuse for being immature. But now fate is calling upon you to deepen your point of view.

Of course you want to succeed in your first job, diligently turning to your boss for assignments, instructions, and guidance, doing everything within your power to carry your projects through to satisfactory completion. You know you are young—and so you defer to your boss with humility and modesty. When you've fallen short of expectations, you summon your earnest desire to improve to try again. Does this sound like what you've been doing?

If you're really in the mess you describe, you have left out the most important piece. The piece you are missing contains the maturity and depth you have been seeking—it contains the secret to ultimate success. However, it comes with a great price attached.

"Everything within your power" includes paying heed to the urgings that come to you from your own heart, your own experience, your own common sense. Paradoxically, in order to progress, you must give these urgings precedence over your desire to please your boss. You are asked to sacrifice your cherished notion of who you are—with your misguided concept of humility and modesty—in favor of taking up the seemingly arrogant stance that even on a new job, even on the very first day, *you matter*. You deserve respect. You are capable and worthy. You stand for something.

99

True humility is the act of surrendering your false notions about yourself—be it arrogance or excessive modesty—to express the whole truth about who and what you are. You give up your misguided efforts to demean yourself in order to please others, and instead set about doing what's right. This is the hero's path. It requires you to be willing to stand alone, shaking in your boots if necessary but holding firm to your course nevertheless. Of course you want your boss to be pleased. But pleasing another must come as a side product of your being true to your own essence and purpose. It must not be allowed to serve as your primary goal.

In fact, even on the very first day of your very first job, you have the right and imperative to give communications that come to you from inside yourself precedence over those that come to you from outside—even when they are issued by your boss. You may have to listen closely for these vital messages, for bosses sometimes speak in very loud voices, while the urgings of your heart, although persistent, are often issued in the tiniest of whispers.

Can you hear the murmurings? That last assignment. You didn't understand it very well, did you? But was that a failure on your part or on your boss's?

Look inside for the answer. If you are not so quick to dismiss yourself in the future, you may find your heart calling you to action the next time you get such an assignment—helping you find the courage to persist with your boss until you are satisfied that you understand exactly what you are to do. If instructions are incomplete, you bravely ask for clarification. When is the assignment due? How long should the report be? Is it important that the copy be centered on the page?

Your boss may become frustrated or impatient with you, but that will not indicate any failure on your part but rather on his. Let the flames issue forth, you will not be turned from your mission.

As you proceed with your work, when questions arise, you seek out further guidance from your boss or other appropriate associates. Use all of the resources you can get your hands on, and if they are insufficient—if, for instance, your boss is unavailable to you and makes no alternate resources available, or if he is curt or unclear with his responses—this is not failure on your part but on his.

If you have done your best—and your gut tells you that given the instructions, information, and guidance that you have received, your best is good enough, at least as a place from which to start—but you and your work are received and judged disrespectfully by your boss, this is not a failure on your part, but on his.

If you offer in good faith to make any necessary corrections, knowing that you are capable of learning from your mistakes, and the assignment is snatched away from you before you are given the opportunity to do so, this is not a failure on your part but on his.

The youth takes the easy road, retreating in self-pity, having failed in his mission to please. He calls this reluctance to defend himself and his willingness to try harder next time modesty and humility. The hero, however, understands that genuine modesty means having the courage to "marshal one's armies even against oneself."

When you follow the path of doing right, you pledge allegiance to a taskmaster far more demanding and difficult to please than any boss you will encounter in all your years of employment: your own heart. Respect yourself first; the rest of your career will take care of itself.

If you love your job but hate your boss, see Tough Business Problem #10.

If you feel that your life is ruined, see Tough Business Problem #100.

TOUGH BUSINESS PROBLEM #9

I've got proposals out to a number of places that may or may not come through. If one does, I'll have it made. If not, it's back to square one. It may be months before everyone responds. Is there anything I can do to reduce my anxiety in the interim?

Periods of transition are fraught with danger.

"What if it should fail, what if it should fail?" Thus has the *I Ching* heard the mournful cry of supplicants for thousands of years. Like it or not, you may not be able to avoid anxiety during this period—but then again, the *I Ching* contends that anxiety is not always a bad thing.

Anxiety demonstrates to you beyond a doubt that you are truly stretching your boundaries to explore new inner terrain. When there is something you really want for yourself—something truly worthy of you—how could you not be anxious? But then you add on to the already elevated level of anxiety inherent in the situation, frightening yourself with thoughts of total success versus abject failure.

In truth, never is the outcome of such a major expenditure of energy and vision as yours an all-or-nothing proposition. The *I Ching* asks you to take comfort from the mulberry bush. When a mulberry bush is cut down, its life is not over. A number of unusually strong shoots sprout from the roots.

In nature destruction often is the requisite state that precedes new growth—be it the felling of a mulberry bush or the bursting open of a pinecone in the heat of a forest fire, which releases its seeds to the newly enriched soil.

Even in your worst-case scenario, there is no way you will find yourself back at square one. The very act of putting the proposal together and of communicating with all your funding sources will have benefited you greatly. You will have new connections, deeper understanding, expanded knowledge as a result of your efforts. You may find yourself somewhere that on the surface looks the same as that place from which you've come, but the truth is that you will have moved ahead, enriched by the growth of your character through the experiences you have undergone in the interim.

Tie your hopes to the roots of the mulberry bush, and while you may not be able to avoid feeling fear, you will—at least—be able to temper your anxiety with sweet anticipation.

If you fear you have to have a positive attitude to get a positive result, see Tough Business Problem #88.

If this situation is keeping you awake nights, see Tough Business Problem #91.

TOUGH BUSINESS PROBLEM #10

I love my job, but I hate my boss. What can I do to transform this situation?

You may aspire to be a master of the universe, ordering life to offer up to you everything you desire. In fact contemporary motivational literature supports you in this belief, advising you not only that you deserve to have it all but that you can have it all.

The reality, however, is that despite how powerful you feel at any given moment—particularly when you are doing a job you love—this universe is quite simply not your show. Although you can certainly have an impact on some of the things that happen to you, there's nothing you can do to get each aspect of your life to turn out for you at any given moment. As the *I Ching* reminds us, life is conditioned and unfree. The superior man surrenders to the concept of limitation—of being able to differentiate between that which he can affect and that which he must accept.

But before you give up on the possibility of ever feeling completely happy again, know this: It is not the fact of limitation that causes you pain; it is rather your willingness to turn against others or yourself when reality fails to live up to your expectations that damages your spirit. It is your injured spirit, not the limitations themselves, that lessen your potential to maximize whatever possibilities for success do come your way.

When facing life's annoyances, such as a boss you hate at a job you love, the challenge is to expand to embrace rather than contract to resist. By embracing your limitations you give your life force direction and velocity. As the philosopher Rollo May suggests, our limitations are like the banks of a river. Without the banks there would be no river.

So rather than using your boss as an excuse to turn against him or yourself, follow an alternate, life-driven approach: Use your boss as an opportunity to turn *for* yourself and others.

How is this possible? In the past when somebody—be it your boss, your big sister, or the neighborhood bully—acted in a way or did something to you that made you angry, sad, defensive, ashamed, or any one of the negative emotions, you saw this as an unpleasant incident you wish could have been avoided. In truth, however, events and individuals who elicit negative emotion from you are providing you access to those aspects of yourself where your potential for increased power, vitality, and creativity have been hidden. Although you may never get to the point where you like your boss, nor may you truly ever eagerly anticipate the pain that life's unpleasant exchanges bring, you may arrive at a greater degree of growth through receptivity to such incidents than you ever thought possible. Try this out for yourself by doing a simple exercise I call "Reclaiming Your Projection." Unpleasant though it is, think of a specific incident that encapsulates for you why you are so filled with negative feelings about your boss. When you've got an incident in mind, answer the following series of questions. Take them one by one as they come—and for maximum impact resist the temptation to peek ahead.

RECLAIMING YOUR PROJECTIONS

1. In relation to this incident, what is the dominant negative quality that your boss embodied? Be as specific as possible.
2. Before you met your boss, who else in your life also carried this negative quality?
3. How have you expressed this negative quality in your own life—either by doing to others (or to yourself) the same thing you dislike in your boss or by bending over backwards to avoid passing it on to others?
4. What do you secretly admire about this quality?
5. What good could come of admitting more of this quality in your life?

A SAMPLE PROJECTION

1. In relation to this incident, what is the dominant negative quality that your boss embodied?

   I work for a man who is extremely judgmental. Nothing I do is ever quite right. He doesn't recognize the great contribution I am already making. I also resent that he has to have things his way all the time.

2. Before you met your boss, who else, in your life also carried this negative quality?

   My older sister had a lot of the responsibility for me. She was really hard on me, the same way my boss is.

3. How have you expressed this negative quality in your own life—either by you doing the same thing you dislike about your boss to others or to yourself, or by bending over backward to avoid passing it on to others?

   I am very hard on myself. I am a perfectionist and I never feel I'm doing as good a job as I should. At the same time the last thing I want to do is impose this on my subordinates. I cut them a lot of slack—maybe too much. I end up cleaning up a lot of their stuff without getting the credit for it.

4. What do you secretly admire about this quality?

   As much as I hate to admit it, I can see that the man I work for is much more courageous than I am. He doesn't apologize for what he wants. I wouldn't like to be him—but I could use more of what he's got: the ability to speak his mind and get what he needs from others without worrying so much about what other people think of him.

5. What good could come of admitting more of this quality in your life?

   I think my productivity would go up because I would spend less of my time and energy cleaning up after others and more time giving my boss what he really wants. Maybe by toughening up with my subordinates I'll be better able to lighten up on myself.

Before you even begin thinking about throwing in the towel on a job you love, go through this five-question process for a month or two every time your boss does something you don't like and see if things don't change radically for you. Confucius said, "When you see a good man, try to emulate his example, and when you see a bad man, search yourself for his faults." When you've gone through the process of accepting and integrating disowned qualities into your life, even the most odious bosses can appear magically transformed into allies.

On the other hand, if after a significant period of time you feel that you've gotten all the gifts this relationship has to offer—and your boss still bugs you—then it's time to think about changing positions. But there's a big surprise waiting for you. For having used this challenge in your life to expand your repertoire of character traits, you will find that you are now able to make your move from a position of strength rather than reactivity. And better yet, having finally completed this stage of growth you will have sufficient clarity and foresight never to work for anyone remotely like your childhood bully again.

If you embrace your negative qualities and alienate your staff, see Tough Business Problem #24.

TOUGH BUSINESS PROBLEM #11

I could do a better job at what my boss is supposed to do than she does. How can I get her job?

You are ambitious. Should you directly challenge your boss? Should you go to your boss's boss? Sign a petition?

But the truth is that feeling one's passion and potential obstructed is not always a bad thing. It can be advantageous to work under such pressure, giving you the time to grow and deepen—like a seed gathering energy beneath the soil. If there were no resistance, your energy could have the misfortune of blossoming prematurely. Out of misguided enthusiasm your true power would be consumed before its time.

Trapped by early success, some people never develop the personal characteristics necessary to rise above whichever stage of development they were in when their success swept them away. Like teenage rock 'n' roll stars, they are stuck playing their first three-chord hit song forever.

How fortunate that you have been given the gift of time—the anvil upon which your character, strengths, abilities, and passion can be forged for purposes beyond what you have imagined for yourself. So what are you to do in the meantime?

Persevere.

"Persevere?" you cry. "You mean to take all my talents, my dreams, my passion—and do nothing?"

Perseverance is the prerequisite for advancement. The *I Ching* teaches that the key to advancement is that "one must first know how to adapt oneself. If a man would rule, he must first learn to serve."

Does learning to serve mean looking the other way when your boss does an inadequate job? Does perseverance mean empty hoping, listless waiting for someone or something to save you? Of course not.

Perseverance as defined by the *I Ching* is simply this: Consistency in doing right. The truly great do not chase after ambition like a dog chasing a cat. Rather they progress by asking themselves the simple question "What is the right thing for me to do next?"

Maintaining a vision for yourself; looking for opportunities to be of service; being accessible and responsive to the opinions and feedback of others, including your boss, while retaining firm principles and a commitment to speaking your truth and doing what's right—these will show you what's next for you.

The great man progresses by "impressing the people so profoundly, by his mere existence and by the impact of his personality, that they will be swayed by him as the grass by the wind." A hidden spiritual power emanates from the great man, influencing and dominating others without his being aware of how it happens.

Your seed is growing stronger each passing day. You can feel it ready to burst through to the sunlight. When your moment has come, nobody will be able to stop you—not an incompetent boss, not an unresponsive system, not lost time or missed opportunities. Nothing.

Do what's right. Do what's next. Heed the summons to act, and when the opportunity to advance presents itself, you will be ready.

If you feel that by biding your time, you are not living up to your potential, see Tough Business Problem #13.

If you feel that it's always right to want to be, have, and do the best, see Tough Business Problem #89.

2

Vision and Purpose

The task is great and full of responsibility. It is nothing less than that of leading the world out of confusion and back to order.

—The *I Ching*

TOUGH BUSINESS PROBLEM #12

I've got a dream that will require my life savings—and probably not support me financially for quite some time. I believe in myself, but something's holding me back from taking the first step. How can I push through my fear?

Contemporary motivational literature teaches us that to win the admiration of your peers—and even hope to catch a whiff of success for yourself—it is your imperative to follow your heart, giving everything you've got (and sometimes more) to achieve your goal. Now, there is no question about whether you should or should not follow your heart. You can always trust your heart. The real question is can you always trust yourself to tell the whole truth about what your heart is asking you to do? In your case, if you were truly to take in the guidance your heart is offering up to you, you'd realize that you are being fervently entreated to take it easy on yourself.

In short, not every fear is meant to be pushed through. Some fears are meant to be heeded and obeyed, at least temporarily.

How can you tell which is which?

The *I Ching* teaches us that if the superior man undertakes something and tries to lead, he goes astray. But if he follows, he finds guidance.

In your desire to push through your fear, are you trying to lead your heart, telling it how and what to feel? Are you denying the wisdom and intuitive knowledge that you carry within you each and every moment of your life? And could it be that this effort to attain your dreams derives more from your ego than from your heart—the desire to see yourself and also be seen as the kind of person who has sufficient faith and trust in himself and the universe to take great risks, when in reality, under these circumstances, you do not?

It is the human condition to be concerned about survival. You have the right to be nervous about the investment of your life's savings with no income in the foreseeable future. Not all ambition is God given. When a man seeks to climb so high that he loses touch with the rest of mankind, he becomes isolated, and this necessarily leads to failure.

In your case I suggest that your fear is the voice of your higher self asking you to take a time-out and see if there might not be some way to accommodate both your dreams and your legitimate concerns. You have the right to both: to be protective of your savings, knowing that you have some way of making a living and/or some savings to fall back upon. And you have the right to pursue your dreams.

This is the middle road . . . the path that has always existed for you, the path that can easily accommodate both your passion and your fears. As your ego ceases to block your view, that way will make itself known to you. And when it does, you will know what it means to follow something with *all* of your heart.

If you are holding off because you want a guarantee that you will do the right thing, see Tough Business Problem #49.

If you push through your fear to take the risk, and your life starts to fall apart around you, see Tough Business Problem #19.

TOUGH BUSINESS PROBLEM #13

With all my so-called potential, why am I not farther along in my career than I am right now?

You have an expectation about where you should be, what you should have achieved by now. Of course you want great things for yourself. And don't you know, you have been progressing at exactly the right pace to achieve them. You have been doing all the right things in all the right ways.

But you have been playing the wrong game.

The universe does not care about your job title or how much money you've earned. The universe cares only for your development as a human being—the strengthening of character traits and a tenacity of spirit that can sustain the highest expression of yourself. The universe cares about qualities such as patience and faith, compassion and forgiveness.

Building character takes time. Here is an invocation to help you remember who you really are:

INVOCATION FOR GREATNESS

The job I am doing now is a small part of what is in store for me.

The real purpose of my work is to provide a forum for the evolution of my spirit, my emotions, my compassion, my patience, and my power.

When I give up my arrogance—my fascination with significance—I see that my everyday life provides many opportunities for such greatness.

When I am taking advantage of what is here now, I will see the path to fulfilling my potential clearly before me.

But I must remember that as I progress, my experience will not be that I am doing something great, but merely, that I am doing what's next.

TOUGH BUSINESS PROBLEM #14

I've been circulating the manuscript for my book to publishers. At this point I've been rejected a dozen times. How long do I keep believing in my book and in myself before throwing in the towel?

Should you persist? The real question you need to ask yourself is if, to the best of your knowledge, you are still being called to the task. Here, even though the creative force is not yet manifesting, the superior man "remains true to himself. He does not allow himself to be influenced by outward success or failure, but, confident in his strength, he bides his time."

If you are truly called to the task, you will be willing to make sacrifices to stay on track with your idea—to get an outside job if your savings have run out, or put your efforts to get published on the back burner temporarily while you take care of other pressing business, knowing that you will get back to it as soon as you are able. You can wait in the calm strength of patience, trusting that time will fulfill its purpose.

The *I Ching* teaches that such patience is not a period of idle waiting but of inner certainty that you have found a vehicle worthy and capable of carrying you on the fastest and most direct route to fulfilling your life purpose.

Sometimes the most direct route to success appears to go in exactly the opposite direction from where you intend to go.

Whereas in Western civilization we are taught that it is effort and will that make things happen, the *I Ching* puts equal stock in releasing and receiving as a viable way to achieve the great success for which you yearn. For instance, while cleaning the floors of a neighbor's house to help pay the bills, temporarily letting go of your driven efforts to get published, you get a creative insight that explains where your manuscript failed to inspire, and how to fix it. Or you end up taking a temporary job—and discover that the husband of a coworker is a literary agent with great connections, anxious to take you on. Or you get a call from an editor who admired your work but was unable to convince the editorial board at his publishing house to take you on; now he tells you that he has since moved to another position and he would like you to resubmit the book if you don't already have a publisher lined up for it.

Though you must always stay focused on your ultimate goal, you must sometimes be willing to put brakes on your strength. If you attempt to obtain by force something for which the time is not yet ripe, you will injure yourself—and perhaps harm your project—by expending your strength prematurely.

It takes great self-discipline and faith to keep your passion burning in your heart when all the circumstances of fate seem to work against you. You must welcome the obstacles you face as you pursue your dream, recognizing that they are the very tools you need to build a foundation strong and stable enough to support the realization of your ultimate purpose.

If you're still game, but your family is begging you to throw in the towel, see Tough Business Problem #42.

If you want to get your book published in order to accomplish something great, see Tough Business Problem #13.

If you persevere and are successful but it doesn't make you happy, see Tough Business Problem #21.

TOUGH BUSINESS PROBLEM #15

For years I had a stable job that bored the heck out of me. Now I've landed a job that is an incredibly exciting opportunity—but the company's financially shaky. Why can't I have it all?

You are feeling sorry for yourself, but the truth is that you should be taking the time to celebrate. You have reached an important milestone in your life.

You are now having higher-quality problems.

If you would like to have it all anyway, see Tough Business Problem #52.

TOUGH BUSINESS PROBLEM #16

I went for stock over higher salary, thinking that my act of faith would pay off. Now the stock is worthless. Where did I go wrong?

Your only error is that you think you have reached the end of something and consider it a failure, whereas in reality you are in the middle of something quite important and exciting. By following your inner voice you have designated yourself for greatness. You are not yet ready to reap the reward, but that is only because where you are truly going is far greater than any future you have yet anticipated for yourself. Anything less—as dazzling as it may seem to you at the time—is an illusion.

An Indian parable tells of a farmer whose crop of wheat suffered first from locusts, then from floods. Although his family had enough to eat, they could not get ahead.

The farmer turned to God and begged for one perfect season: "God—send me plenty of sunshine and just the right amount of rain, no pests, and a gentle breeze. That's all I ask."

God obliged, and the farmer watched his new crop of wheat grow strong and tall. He fell on his knees to offer his thanks to God, but in the distance he heard his wife and children cry out. They had torn open the beautiful husks and found them empty. Without resistance the wheat had failed to produce its seed.

Still on his knees, the farmer continued, "But next year, God, send me just enough troubles to make my wheat strong."

You are like the farmer. You wish you didn't have troubles. But it is these very difficulties that ensure the development of character and personality strong enough to support the greater destiny that awaits you.

Knowing that you have a greater destiny in store for you does not take away from your sadness and frustration. It is natural and perhaps even important to feel bad about your apparent losses along the way. But greatness belongs to him who, in addition to his distress, finds it in his heart to feel grateful for troubles. He alone remembers that all you can ever really lose is your illusions.

If losing a year's wheat crop is nothing compared with the disaster you're facing, see Tough Business Problem #53.

TOUGH BUSINESS PROBLEM #17

I'm thinking of following my passion back to school to train for a new career. But at my age, with my responsibilities and obligations, am I being realistic?

You'd like to pursue your dream without making a sacrifice? You'd like to preserve your standard of living and not ask anything of your family and friends in terms of additional support? You feel the urge to be realistic?

Of course you must pay attention to these issues. But before we deal with the logistical aspects of your situation, take a moment to appreciate fully how fortunate you are that you have found something you'd love to do. What a great gift has been given to you—sent to you from the primal depths of the universe!

Your willingness to shoulder responsibilities over the years demonstrates that you already know how to make a living, how to be a responsible member of the community. You have already mastered stability. Now you have been shown the path to your heart. You are at a new level of growth and development. Here your task is to master chaos.

Times of growth are beset with difficulties. But these difficulties arise from the very profusion of all that is struggling to attain form. Difficulties at the beginning are too great for some people. The *I Ching* portrays these individuals as folding their hands and giving up the struggle. Confucius says that such resignation is the saddest of all things—the shedding of bloody tears.

Are you shedding bloody tears as you speak of making a "decent living," of "taking a more realistic approach." Is it living at all to deny your dreams in order to be secure? Is reality offering you stability as the booby prize for contemplating giving up what you most love to do? Or can you find it within yourself to take a leap of faith

121

to a whole new universe—one that holds the promise of a far greater experience of happiness and success than you have ever achieved in the stable life of yours that came before?

"A decent living"—what does it really take to support yourself when your joy and sustenance come from allowing your creative process to unfold unhindered by fears about what other people think? How much of your living wage is spent compensating for the sacrifice of your spirit? How much of your livelihood is devoted to protecting yourself and isolating yourself from others? Now it is time to join in community: to pool resources, to find alternate ways of providing or sharing goods and services.

"A realistic approach"—the arrogant presumption that you know what reality is and what it demands of you. You have only one reality you can count on—your own heart that is begging you to pursue what you love.

Success is already yours. But to recognize this, you will have to make a sacrifice. You must confess that your old ways—calling the shots, protecting your ego, playing it safe, doing it on your own—no longer work for you. You must give up the idea that you are in control.

Your rational mind rebels. What your heart is telling you doesn't make sense. And yet it persists, whispering to you over and over again that there is a new way to live.

Can you trust that you will be all right? That you can follow your heart and be assured that the universe will not abandon you?

Recently I led a workshop at Omega Institute with Vicki Robin, coauthor with Joe Dominguez of *Your Money or Your Life*, and Denise Breton and Christopher Largent, authors of *The Soul of Economies*. Vicki and Joe advocate and teach a practical, hands-on process by which individuals align the way they actually spend their time and money with their deeper values. They make a convincing case for the connection between what is written on the pages of your checkbook register and the state of our planet. Many individuals who work their steps come to understand that many of the things we aspire to own, have, do, and be are not only not necessities, but may not even be consistent with our own deeply held values. Working consciously, they begin to reevaluate what are the things they must keep in their lives—medical insurance, for example, and some kind of roof over their heads—and what they can release—a second car, for instance, or perhaps even both their cars, or expensive steak dinners.

Listening to Vicki, I was reminded of a favorite Thoreau-inspired story in which two men set out for a nearby town. The first chooses to go on foot. It takes him most of a day to get there. He arrives invigorated by his walk, breathing in the air around him deeply and singing all the way.

The second has a car. He does not arrive until the following day—a full day later than the one who walked. Why? Because first he had to work a day at a job he couldn't stand to pay for the gas to get him there. He arrives surrounded by fumes and muttering bitterly under his breath about his rotten life.

As full of information and enthusiasm as the presenters were, the greatest teachings came from the dozens of stories that emerged over the course of the weekend from the attendees. It soon became apparent that among us were a great many who had taken the leap of faith to follow their hearts—freeing themselves from financial obligations and material considerations that once dominated their lives. I especially remember the vibrant couple who bought a year's sabbatical from unsatisfying careers by trading in their suburban home, isolated by yards and fences, for the enriched intimacy of less "privileged" neighborhoods with street life. They got the time and space that they needed to reevaluate their career paths. And there was a side benefit as well. In their new neighborhood, free for the asking, they discovered the sense of community and wholeness they had previously been seeking through expensive therapies and retreats.

Several individuals told of following the practical techniques suggested by Vicki and Joe to cut their family's living expenses from fifty and even a hundred thousand dollars or more a year to ten, fifteen, or twenty-five thousand. Many were working towards—and an increasing number of cases had reached—the goal of financial independence.

It can be done.

It will take patience to sort out the knotty challenge that has presented itself to you. But the *I Ching* teaches us that "in order to find one's place in the infinity of being, one must be able both to separate and to unite."

Separate from your old ways of working and living, unite with others of like mind. In time you will find that you have more than it takes to bind your passion into skeins.

If you want to proceed but fear is holding you back, see Tough Business Problem #12.

If you want to proceed but your coworkers are discouraging you, see Tough Business Problem #57.

TOUGH BUSINESS PROBLEM #18

I've developed a foolproof plan guaranteed to make me millions, and I am going to do whatever it takes to succeed. Nothing is going to get in my way. The trouble is that so far the venture capitalists keep passing up this great opportunity. What's wrong with them?

Perhaps it is time to stop looking for fault in these venture capitalists, whom you consider blind to the truth, and instead explore another possibility. Is it possible that they hesitate because they intuit that your resolve, while admirable in its intent, may fail you when the going gets tough?

How could this be? The *I Ching* explains that when a man endeavors to soar above all obstacles, proclaiming, as you have, to let nothing get in the way, he encounters a hostile fate. Rather than making himself ready to flow around and over the obstacles any worthwhile endeavor is destined to encounter, he becomes brittle and reactive. He sets himself against the universe, inadvertently increasing rather than decreasing resistance by the nature of his arrogant stance.

A more productive affirmation is to proclaim that you are going to do whatever it takes to succeed, even as you accept that *many* things are going to get in your way. This funding problem is but the first of many. If you are prepared only for advance—and not for retreat—you will soon exhaust your resources.

Rather than attack your career as if it were an enemy to be conquered, take your inspiration from water. As the *I Ching* says, "Water sets the example for right conduct under such circumstances. It flows on and on, and merely fills up all the places through which it flows; it does not shrink from any dangerous spot nor from any plunge, and nothing can make it lose its own essential nature. It remains true to itself under all conditions."

125

As Confucius said, "If a man can just for one day realize his true self, and restore complete moral discipline, the world will follow him. To be a true man depends on yourself. What has it got to do with others?"

The apparent rejection you are suffering now is in reality teaching you exactly what you need to know in order to proceed over the long haul without becoming depleted in the end. When you have completed this learning, you will be someone worth investing in. You will find an investor.

If you are wondering what to do with yourself in the interim, see Tough Business Problem #9.

If you think that if you are smart enough, hard-working enough, and good enough, you will have it all, see Tough Business Problem #52.

TOUGH BUSINESS PROBLEM #19

I followed my heart, and now everything is falling apart around me. I still feel that I did and am doing the right thing. How can I hold all this apparent failure without letting it take me under?

THE HERO'S INVOCATION

The hero follows his heart, knowing that there are no guarantees that he will get the result he thinks he wants, when and how he wants it.

Why, then, should you follow the hero's way? Because the alternative is to abandon yourself. Though you feel terrible right now, you can't truly know how this situation is going to turn out in the end.

In the meantime you can blame others or yourself for your bad luck; or you can invest in expensive counseling to explain and attempt to minimize the damage. But Joseph Campbell, who wrote so eloquently on the hero, suggests this course: "To handle the life that arises."

Feel grateful that you know your heart well enough to follow it; feel humble that you have the grace of holding firm to your conviction that you did and are doing the right thing.

As for the rest, here's an invocation that you can use to help you evoke the participation of your will at this changing time:

May I remember that the price for going for what I truly believe in at first seems always greater than what I am willing to pay ... but isn't.

The solid structures that served as my bridge, giving me a way to traverse from the old to the new, crumble beneath my feet with every quickening step assuring that there will be no turning back.

As I cross over, may I find the strength to hold on to my faith, loosening the grip on my external reality, watching in awe and amazement as the old structures reconfigure around my unwavering conviction.

If you believe that by having an unwavering conviction, nothing is going to get in your way, see Tough Business Problem #18.

If it's taking too long for your taste for your world to reconfigure around your convictions, see Tough Business Problem #99.

TOUGH BUSINESS PROBLEM #20

After years of struggle I am receiving the adulation and support for my work I always thought I deserved. But now that the demand is there, I've never felt less inspired. How can I regain my enthusiasm?

When you were on your own, you had only your faith to light the way through the darkness. Because of this you tended your spirit diligently—and so it showed you the way to success.

Now that you stand in the spotlight of the admiration of many, perhaps you have allowed your own light to dim. The *I Ching* warns that danger lurks at the place of transition from lowliness to the heights: "Many a great man has been ruined because the masses flocked to him and swept him into their course."

In place of genuine inspiration, you have entangled yourself in the greatest folly: imitation of yourself. You have taken the short-cut to happiness, allowing money and fame to supply you with the sense of self-respect you once provided for yourself. Not only that, you sense deep in your bones that what has been given to you by others could as easily be taken away by others.

The antidote: Take a new risk. Reconnect to your unique passion—the voice that sounded alone for so long and that still beckons to you to heed its call. It's still inside you, whispering to you, but you have stopped listening to it and started listening to the others.

So take a risk! You owe it to yourself and to the world to do something fresh, new, unexpected, daring—something that tests or challenges those who have laid claim to you. Don't do it for sensation's sake, for the purpose of upsetting those around you. Do it rather, to reconnect to your unique voice and heart. Feel the adrenaline pulse; let your heart race!

Continue to express the real essence of yourself; that will be revolutionary enough—for each and every one of us, when freed to show our true selves, is full of the unexpected.

If you hope to make the transition from lowliness to the heights, there is only one way: You must be willing to lose it all.

If you feel that no matter how much you achieve, something's still not quite right, see Tough Business Problem #99.

If you fear that if you take the risk of changing, you will disappoint your supporters, see Tough Business Problem #61.

If you push on despite the fact that your passion is gone, hoping for the best, see Tough Business Problem #62.

TOUGH BUSINESS PROBLEM #21

I've finally completed my project, achieving a lifelong goal, but instead of feeling elated, I'm depressed. What should I do?

Set a bigger goal.

TOUGH BUSINESS PROBLEM #22

Faced with obstacles too great for me to surmount, I'm filing for bankruptcy. The financial burden is bad enough, but what's worse is the knowledge that my dream failed. How can I ever hope to recover from this?

A Buddhist monk, seeking the key to enlightenment, sat still in contemplation in the temple garden. As he sat, a maple leaf broke free from a tree nearby and floated gently to the ground.

The monk bowed in homage to the leaf that had showed him how effortlessly it shared both its front and its back side as it fell, hiding nothing. No self-consciousness, no fear, no embarrassment or regret.

So should we be with our perceived failures, seeing the back side of our efforts as an integral part of the whole.

How can you be this accepting, this much at peace?

The answer is by having faith in the greater picture—a deep-seated understanding that in order for the tree of life to renew itself in spring, the leaves must fall in the autumn.

Here is an invocation that you can use to help recover your faith:

INVOCATION FOR NEW BEGINNINGS

All that is truly meant to be mine will be returned to me in time.
Even if I fear I don't deserve it.
Even if I have thrown it away.

May I remember that any moment can be a turning point.
I can begin anew the moment I envision the best rather than worst potential outcome.

Although I find this difficult right now, I can make myself receptive to new possibilities that arise from outside my existing expectations and experiences, trusting that everything that happens to me has a purpose.

From my limited perspective, I see only the small patch of darkness surrounding me. But even here, I can have faith. For my willingness to invoke my higher self shines like a beacon of light showing the way through the darkness quenching my regret with the comforting thought:

Where else but in the dark could light shine?

If you feel you just don't have it in you to try again, see Tough Business Problem #100.

3

Managing Others

By contemplating the forms existing in the heavens we come to understand time and its changing demands. Through contemplation of the forms existing in human society it becomes possible to shape the world.

—The *I Ching*

TOUGH BUSINESS PROBLEM #23

I gave my assistant a tedious assignment that, frankly, I was happy I wouldn't have to do. When I did, I thought I saw resentment flash across her face. Is it honesty or intrusion to share what I saw?

In the heat of the moment it isn't always easy to know what is the honest response. Here's a process that you can put to work for you:

When you think you see resentment or anger on someone's face, check your reaction. Are you responding emotionally? Are you angry? Afraid? When you are reactive to an event, only the part of you that is fearful and angry gets to talk. That voice may not be the most appropriate one for this particular circumstance, no matter how justified it may seem to be at the time. Given that this may be the case, you are not ready to take action.

Temporarily place your emotions and judgments on hold while you gather sufficient information to make an objective assessment of the situation. Are you sure you read the look of resentment accurately? Ask in a neutral tone if your subordinate has a problem with the assignment. The response itself may resolve your problem—for example, she may say "No, I'm having gas cramps."

If at this point the situation does not resolve itself to your satisfaction—for example, she says she has no problem with the assignment, but her tone of voice or body language says otherwise—and you are still charged emotionally, you are still not yet ready to take action. You will want to call for a time-out to sort through this further on your own.

In a business relationship in which you hold authority, it is rarely appropriate to speak your inner process out loud or to work it out with your coworkers. Using your staff as a therapy group would be an indulgence. Resist the temptation. Instead, without excusing or de-

136

fending yourself, obtain the time you need by saying, "I'm uncomfortable with your response, but I am not at a point where I can spend time talking this through with you right now. Go ahead and finish up, and we can continue this conversation later."

Now it is time to ask yourself a potentially painful question: "What is the unspoken fear about myself that this incident has tapped into? That I'm not respected? That I'm unworthy of respect?"

Are you afraid this person doesn't respect you? Telling the whole truth means being willing to look at the places you've fallen short in your own expectations for yourself—and committing yourself to correcting what you can. But, just as importantly, telling the whole truth also means giving yourself credit for what you do well.

You can't begin to get perspective on what is going on with others until you've got a pretty good idea of what is going on with you. When you are willing and able to make an honest assessment of yourself, you will find a more stable place from which to act.

What I believe you may find in this particular case—the case of the tedious assignment—is that you were actually feeling guilty and apprehensive about giving your subordinate the assignment in the first place. That doesn't mean you aren't justified in dealing with your subordinate's resentment or that you should not have given her the assignment. But it does mean that you will deal with this situation more effectively once you have sorted out the personal issues that have little or nothing to do with this particular incident.

Now it's time to act. Guided by your understanding of your own motives, you will know what to say and do. And give yourself credit for putting yourself in a position of power and authority, where you are bound to be brought face-to-face not only with other people's inner demons but your own as well.

If your assistant's look of resentment is not an isolated incident, see Tough Business Problem #24.

If you don't trust your assistant, see Tough Business Problem #31.

TOUGH BUSINESS PROBLEM #24

The word at the water cooler is that my subordinates generally dislike me. They think I don't care about them, when the truth is I'm simply serious about doing a good job. Without lowering my standards, how can I turn public opinion around?

Confucius's most devoted disciple asked of his teacher, "What would you say if all the people of the village like a person?"

Confucius replied, "That is not enough."

"What would you say if all the people of the village dislike a person?"

"That is not enough," said Confucius, explaining, "It is better when the good people of the village like him and the bad people of the village dislike him."

Being liked is highly overrated in the corporate environment. Being respected is a far more important attribute. If it is passion for your work rather than fear that is fueling your seriousness, then more power to you. We need more heroism in the workplace—individuals who are willing to take a stand, even though it upsets the status quo. Your courage and conviction are to be admired.

On the other hand, there is no need to set yourself up for negative opinion if it could easily be averted by some low-key personal public relations. For instance, taking the time for such niceties as "thank you" and "please" may seem like an unnecessary energy drain to a hard-charging individual like you. But there is a place for the social graces in the workplace. If your concern is for the good of your company—not just your own personal efforts at time management—you will realize that the time and energy it takes to integrate pleasantness into your daily interactions more than offsets the time previously spent by disgruntled subordinates mumbling about you to one another in the hallways.

Another worthwhile investment of your time and energy is taking a few moments after a subordinate's weekend, vacation, or absence of any sort to express interest or concern, as the occasion merits. Hopefully you are not so totally invested in productivity that you can't actually muster some genuine feelings about the people with whom you work. If so, it is better to fake it than to do nothing. But if you find that you do need to fake it, you will want to take a deeper look at the issues the water-cooler gossip has uncovered.

For instance, how and why is it that you've made your work so important—and the people you work with so unimportant? Could it be that work is something you can count on to be reliable, something that you can control to a greater extent than the human beings in your life? Yes, there is risk in opening yourself to interaction with others, even if the opening is as tiny a crack as a heartfelt greeting in the morning. When you give to others, you make a space to receive. Do you fear that along with whatever goodies that may come your way, there will be demands made upon you and your time that you aren't prepared to meet? Are you afraid a little genuine civility will open Pandora's box, that you will discover that you have very little expertise in handling two-way conversations, in receiving feedback, or in setting mature limits?

Often the person in the organization who is least willing to take on the risks of personal interaction with others is ironically the person who apparently holds the most power: the boss. But what better place to hide out from your fears of intimacy and vulnerability than at the top of the totem pole? The higher you get in the traditional pyramid, the more you get to give orders and get your needs met—without having to worry about being confronted with any kind of real feedback that might actually require you to feel pain or to change how you interact with the world. And you isolate yourself further by feeling superior to those who are apparently bringing "less" to the workplace than you.

But the *I Ching* teaches that the great leader should not set himself above his troops: "The leader should be in the midst of his army, in touch with it, sharing good and bad with the masses he leads. This alone makes him equal to the heavy demands made upon him."

You could be in bigger trouble than you've imagined if your subordinates intuit that your seriousness comes coupled with critical judgments about their "less serious" attitudes.

To rejoin your troops, you will have to bring new thinking to the situation. Consider these possibilities:

Could it be that your subordinates are not bringing "less to work with them every day"—just something different? Perhaps they realize that in the context of their workday they actually accomplish more if they have a positive feeling not only about the work to be done but about the people with whom they work. Perhaps they are more willing to take risks in their relationships, so the easy interaction with others does not represent the energy and time drain to them that it does to you. Perhaps they have a firmer grasp on the ultimate goal of work: to serve the community, understanding that community consists not of work accomplished but of people—not only those individuals outside the company but those inside as well. Although they may be in a less demanding and/or rewarding position in the pyramid than you are, perhaps your subordinates have actually been able to find meaning in their friendships that the work itself has not provided.

If they are doing a decent job, the burden to avert disaster is on you. Can you grow to encompass the diversity and to appreciate the more human elements of working with others?

If your subordinates are functioning adequately on behalf of your company, they deserve your respect. Can you find it in your heart to appreciate the nobility of the human spirit, the willingness to reach out to one another in an earnest effort to deal with the bittersweet realities of life?

Only when your answer is yes will you begin to develop the most serious and ultimately the most productive character trait of all, the character trait that is at the root of all respect, that is better than commitment, better than loyalty, better than efficiency.

You will develop compassion for the human condition.

If you wait too long and your staff organizes against you, see Tough Business Problem #22.

If you try to treat your staff more compassionately and things blow up in your face, see Tough Business Problem #19.

TOUGH BUSINESS PROBLEM #25

My secretary does his job well enough—and he's pleasant and well-meaning. But he has bad dandruff. I've suggested he seek medical treatment, and it's somewhat improved, but I still notice it. Nobody else seems to be bothered by it. What should I do?

Just as the earth is able to carry and preserve all things that live and move upon it, so the superior man is big enough to support imperfection.

The key here is not to attempt to focus on what your assistant should do to grow toward perfection, but for you to grow to encompass everything that transpires, including his imperfection. You see everything—while choosing to let many things pass. The superior man is capable of doing this because his inner concentration and depth of character allow him to differentiate between the trivial and the vital.

The next time you are bothered by your secretary's dandruff, turn your judgment to gratitude. How fortunate you are to be given the opportunity to expand each and every workday!

If you are overwhelmed by this problem, see Tough Business Problem #84.

TOUGH BUSINESS PROBLEM #26

I have worked hard to make my workplace reflective of the things I value, qualities such as honesty and integrity. When interviewing prospective employees, I try to make it clear that I "walk my talk." So why can't I find or keep a good secretary?

What you have done is raised the stakes for what you expect out of your relationships. You want and deserve to have individuals who support you and your company out of a sense of service, without resentment or arrogance; who are enthusiastic, honest, and mature.

It's easier to find people who can type and file.

Why is this so? You are up against a culture that has largely produced a talent pool of individuals who got their training in traditional hierarchies. In shut-down environments people are taught to hide out in the woodworks of poor communications channels; the real dialogue in these old-paradigm structures takes place in the form of gossip and backstabbing. As long as you do your job and take care not to rock the boat, you are left largely alone.

Now, in your environment of open communications, you present them with a new challenge: to rise to the occasion, trusting that honesty will be rewarded rather than punished. Not everyone wants to work in an environment that values these qualities. In fact some people prefer shut-down environments, where they will be better able to hide their negative attitudes. Others think they might enjoy working in a life-driven environment, but realize after taking the job, that being in a situation that asks that they do what it takes to have honest and straightforward relationships requires more of them than they'd anticipated.

Whereas it is possible to screen out obvious mismatches in the interview process, it can take anywhere from one day to three months on the job to discover that a candidate isn't a good fit. For that reason I suggest you establish a "no-fault" trial period, during which either of you can terminate the relationship for any reason with no fallout to either party. Let your employee know that this no-fault trial works both ways: that he or she can give notice during this period for any or even no reason, at any time during this period.

A bonus of this escape-hatch approach is that it allows you to take risks on individuals who hold sufficient promise to give it a go, but who might not previously have made the grade. Some individuals who start out cautious and suspicious of your culture may well begin to thrive once trust has been built.

If you can keep your standards high while lowering the risk factor, you might find that extra bit of luck you've been searching for.

If you let your last secretary go because he had bad dandruff, see Tough Business Problem #25.

If your top candidate passes on your offer and goes to work for a company that abuses its employees, see Tough Business Problem #63.

TOUGH BUSINESS PROBLEM #27

How do I handle the fact that one of my key subordinates ignores our professional, corporate environment and insists on wearing saddle shoes to meetings with clients?

Do you have the right to set and enforce standards in your workplace? In fact, as a manager with subordinates, isn't this in fact your responsibility?

In the healthy organization the leader gains the confidence and obedience of his subordinates by coming to stand for something. You are the living representation of your division's standards, purpose, and devotion to duty. This spans the gamut of responsibilities—from delineating and maintaining a vision for your group to making sure that the clothing and appearance of your subordinates do not become a distraction for coworkers and clients.

So you feel petty putting all this attention on something as silly as saddle shoes, right? If you've already broached the subject, your subordinate has probably talked to you about freedom and creativity and self-expression. By now you may be feeling downright un-American for bringing up the ridiculous issue.

But recognize that this situation is not about saddle shoes. In truth it is not even about your subordinate. If it were, you would simply say, "Saddle shoes are not appropriate attire in a corporate setting. Wear what you like on your own time, but for client meetings please select something more suitable," and that would be that.

No, the real issue at stake here is leadership. Your leadership.

The *I Ching* teaches us that in order to inspire enthusiastic compliance from your troops, you must first be collected within yourself. You must be a firm center around which your subordinates may gather.

That said, you must now consider the source of your reluctance to

144

act on this matter. It is possible, for instance, that you secretly agree with your subordinate. Maybe what you want to say is, "By golly, there's no reason why we shouldn't be able to wear saddle shoes to client meetings. I'm going to back you up on this one."

If this is the case, remember one important piece of advice before you act: pick your battles carefully. Sooner or later, there will come a time when you will be willing to buck the entire system to achieve something vital. Is the right to wear saddle shoes really the issue on which you are willing to stake your career?

It may well be. For instance, the saddle shoes may be the physical manifestation of deeper problems within your company—is yours a repressive environment in which creativity and personal expression are routinely squashed for no good purpose? If this is the case, the saddle shoes may well represent a cause worth fighting for.

On the other hand, if your company is doing just fine, then what is the significance of the saddle shoes? They could be your key employee's unconscious strategy for finding his way out of your company and back to art school.

One thing is certain: If you keep asking the right questions, there will come a moment when you know for sure what the saddle shoes mean to you.

If you take your stand against the saddle shoes and the whole division rallies behind their coworker and against you, see Tough Business Problem #24.

If your subordinate stops wearing the saddle shoes but develops a bad case of dandruff, see Tough Business Problem #25.

If you are the one wearing the saddle shoes, see Tough Business Problem #52.

TOUGH BUSINESS PROBLEM #28

I used to enjoy my work, but the company just hired someone whose very tone of voice is driving me crazy— and her desk is right next to mine! Every day she comments on whether she likes what I'm wearing, eavesdrops on my conversations, and does a zillion other irritating things. I talked to my supervisor, but he said I have to make the best of this situation. Help!

Assuming that you've also taken up the issue directly with her with little or no success, you are facing one of those moments when you have no recourse but to admit helplessness. You can't change the situation—and you don't want to quit. You've only got one other option: You'll have to change yourself.

What if you could change yourself in such a way that you could remain at your desk and continue to enjoy your job, with this abrasive person just feet from you?

The *I Ching* teaches that when you are stuck in a pit, inner composure is your only recourse. Here's one way to restore inner composure when under duress. The next time she bothers you, take a moment to visualize yourself sitting at your desk. Beneath you are thousands of rose petals. You pick the color. Pink offers serenity. White offers simplicity and purity. Red offers vitality.

Go ahead—indulge yourself. Now, imagine a magic square surrounding your desk. In each corner visualize a rosebush. Take a good look. What shape are your rosebushes in? Are the flowers in full bloom? Leaves shiny and green? If you can still hear your nemesis's voice through the bushes, they are not lush enough. Are they wilted? Petals dropping? Turning black? Plump up your bushes visually. When they are in full bloom, you will be fully protected.

See, you can even smile at her through rose petals. She can see you, while you can easily screen out her annoying habits. Decorum is maintained.

If she manages to penetrate your space with a direct question or comment, arrange a pleasant but vaguely blank expression on your face, then give her an all-purpose response, inspired by Miss Manners, good for just about any situation, such as "How nice for you."

"I hate the blouse you're wearing today. It clashes with your skirt."

"How nice for you."

"I heard that you are planning to go to Old Joe's for lunch. I was there yesterday and it stinks."

"How nice for you."

If her voice starts getting to you again as the day progresses, take a look at your bushes. Have you left them untended to droop and wilt? Then take a moment to plump them up again.

The *I Ching* explains that when handling wild, intractable people, one's purpose will best be achieved if one behaves with decorum.

"Pleasant manners succeed even with irritable people."

How nice for you.

If you feel the urge to help this person by giving her the name of a good therapist, see Tough Business Problem #40.

TOUGH BUSINESS PROBLEM #29

I get the feeling that my business associate doesn't respect me, but I have no idea why. If I address this head-on, won't I be opening up a can of worms?

In the theater of the workplace the pantomime of relationship is often played out in subtle gestures of avoidance. Heavy sighs, eyes turned heavenward, a pregnant void in place of a "hello" or "thank you." Boss or employee, client or associate, you fight a silent enemy—the problem not on the surface begging for resolution. The entire corporate culture becomes mired in gestures that somehow manage to hang untended, like loose threads, never to be addressed head-on. We fear pulling at even the tiniest bit of cloth, in the sometimes-justified belief that if we do, the fabric may unravel. Intuitively you may realize that the disrespectful associate represents a bigger problem, something about yourself that will be uncomfortable to confront—something that you will have to change.

Perhaps what you will have to change is your willingness to have business associates who treat you disrespectfully. Do you have the courage to demand respect? Perhaps you are unsure if you are really worthy of respect or not. If you do act on your own behalf, you wonder, will there be any new relationships that will come to take the place of the old? Will you be abandoned, putting your business dealings in jeopardy? Is your very survival threatened?

If you are to run your career and your organization on spiritual principles, however, you must be willing to follow the loose threads wherever they may lead. Although it is true that your constructions may unravel because you have chosen to start asking difficult questions, the truth is that such constructions most probably would have unraveled on their own sooner or later anyway. The only question is whether you want to be in a position to be an active participant in the unravelling process or to be a victim of it.

Stacy, a good friend of mine, makes spare change as a part-time fashion consultant. She helps women upgrade their wardrobes in a two-part process. For the first part Stacy goes to her client's home to help her to sort through the clothes in her closet, selecting those items worth keeping and discarding those that don't work particularly well. For the second part Stacy takes her client shopping to help her select items to fill in the holes in her wardrobe.

My friend is great at what she does, but she refers to it as her hobby and is very insecure about herself in the professional role. When I called her recently for a friendly check-in, I found her deeply depressed.

She had just spent an uncomfortable evening with a new client who had been referred by a mutual friend. Stacy perceived the woman as being much wealthier and more stylish than most of her other clients and felt fearful about her competence under the circumstances. To top things off, the woman resisted many of Stacy's suggestions. While disrespect was implied rather than stated, Stacy left feeling that she had failed miserably.

Stacy told me she was sure it was because of the clothing she herself had chosen to wear to the woman's house. Perhaps the outfit she'd chosen for the professional outing was too informal. The woman obviously hadn't taken her seriously. Because she did not work at it full-time, Stacy felt like an amateur—a fake. This woman had clearly seen right through her.

As she poured out her tale of woe, "call waiting" interrupted us for an extended moment. When Stacy returned, embarrassment oozed over the line.

It had been her client. The woman was indeed upset—but not because she felt she'd wasted her money on Stacy's services. She was upset because Stacy had left without setting a time and date for the second part of the process.

Stacy realized that she invariably took any client's mood personally—as if it always meant something specific about her own failings and insecurities. It was a kind of reverse arrogance, a grandiose notion of the importance of her impact on other people's lives. She realized that the woman's resistance to her suggestions was not resentment but the normal reluctance to part with favorite clothing that many of her less well-heeled clients felt as well.

I spoke with Stacy sometime after this incident. She reported to me that the second session had gone off without a hitch, mostly because she had learned to do a couple of new things. First of all, she took special care to dress for the occasion and present herself in a manner more in keeping with her own high standards. But even more importantly, when the woman ignored her first couple of suggestions and appeared to Stacy to walk off in a huff, she found the courage to ask, "I notice you aren't taking many of my suggestions. Are you upset with me about something?"

The woman was chagrined that her overly efficient style had been mistaken for upset, and the incident actually broke the ice in their relationship. The woman has since referred a number of clients to Stacy, who discovered that what was hidden in her own can of worms was the secret to turning her part-time hobby into a full-time career.

Stacy commented to me later that even if her worst fears had come true, the incident would still have been a gift. The issue of her professionalism had been haunting her for some time. This was her opportunity to confront the issue head-on and do something about it one way or the other.

Whatever you find in your own can of worms, the following invocation will help you get the respect you desire.

INVOCATION FOR BETTER WORKING RELATIONSHIPS

I am grateful for this disrespectful relationship that has served me by strengthening my resolve to be worthy of and to demand respect in my life.

I have taken my stand, and now, I put the recovery of my working relationships in the universe's hands, knowing that there will be a "what's next for me" that acknowledges how far I've come and how much respect I deserve.

As painful as it sometimes is, I am grateful for the process of my life and for the ever-expanding clarity and insight it brings to me benefiting all aspects of my life.

If this relationship is not an isolated incident, see Tough Business Problem #60.

If you demand respect in your relationships and your life starts to unravel around you, see Tough Business Problem #19.

If you're wondering if expressing your true feelings to your associate is the honest thing to do, see Tough Business Problem #23.

TOUGH BUSINESS PROBLEM #30

My secretary is hopeless—and he's the boss's nephew. I am trying to be charitable, but I can't trust myself to hold my tongue any longer. What should I do?

In the name of surrender and acceptance you are attempting to close the gap between illusion and reality with your own fear-driven efforts. By keeping still about the issue, you are serving no one but your own self-interests.

Do you call this charity? What kind of a gift are you giving to the nephew, who is being prevented by you from having to confront his own weaknesses? You are stealing from him the opportunity to learn and grow. Is it his pain you are thinking about—or your own?

You must believe that the universe offers support and purpose for everyone, just as it does for you. It would be arrogant to believe that while you have the right and obligation to ask questions and receive feedback guiding you to the fulfillment of your destiny, others do not. In this case we are talking about both the hopeless nephew and his charitable uncle. They are just as worthy—and just as capable of fulfilling their potential—as you, whether they know it or not.

Your boss has put you and his nephew in a situation where you all are being asked to deviate from your own true natures. You are squashing your spirit to cover up another's weakness; the nephew is being shielded from the growth that comes from confronting reality. And your boss—can he be managing his company best to serve the needs of the greater community if the organization has built weakness and pity into the fabric of its structure?

Until you have found it within yourself to confront this situation with compassion, courage, and honesty, calling another person hopeless is more a reflection of your arrogance than of his ability to fulfill his potential—working for you or elsewhere in the company or the world. You will understand the true meaning of service when you find it within yourself to make a contribution to another that is driven by something more worthy of you than self-interest and fear.

If you do the courageous thing, and the nephew ends up with your job, see Tough Business Problem #53.

TOUGH BUSINESS PROBLEM #31

My employee acts as if I'm bugging him when I'm simply following up on projects I've delegated. What's going on here?

You would like your employee to honor your authority, to believe, as you do, that you have a legitimate right to monitor his responsibilities. And that right is indeed yours. But he feels something in addition to your desire for respect—he feels your lack of trust.

Is he right? If you don't trust him, then stop just treating the symptoms by pushing or pulling his projects to completion; instead dig in to do the hard work of ferreting out the truth about your relationship to him. Even more than having the right to check up on your employee's progress, you have the right to have an employee you can trust. And more important still, you have the right to be a trusting individual.

Where does one begin? Try granting your employee the benefit of the doubt on his next assignment in order to see how he performs when you act from a position of trust rather than fear with him.

Even if you have to clean up a mess here and there along the way, it is far better to err on the side of being too trusting with your employees than being too suspicious.

Why? Confucius teaches that things that accord in tone vibrate together. "Things that have affinity in their inmost nature seek one another. Water flows to what is wet, fire turns to what is dry."

And so it follows that trustworthy people flow to him who is trusting, and—the bad news—untrustworthy people flow to the suspicious. If you are surrounded by untrustworthy people, you may have to do a fair bit of soul-searching before you are ready to take up the discussion with your employee. What are your issues with trust? Do they really have to do with this particular employee? Or do they go back to an earlier stage in your life? Can you begin to see that this is not all about getting your employee to act less bugged, but about learning how you can establish a healthier relationship to trust? If it's too much to take a leap of faith, then start with a baby step.

Here's how to begin. The manager who has a healthy relationship with trust knows how to set limits and how to build upon his subordinates' successes along the way. Make sure the next assignment you delegate to your employee is one in which the potential for failure falls within an acceptable range of risk for you.

Give the assignment, then discipline yourself not to check up on him until it is due. Cold turkey.

If and as the employee proves himself worthy of your trust by completing the project to your satisfaction, increase the responsibility delegated on the next project. In the best-case scenario you will be back to your original level of supervision within an assignment or two—but without the shadow of mistrust looming over both of you.

If the discomfort persists, you may have to look at another related issue. For another element of faith has to do with whether your employee trusts that he can come to you should he have problems with an assignment.

Can he? Or are you a perfectionist who believes everybody should be able to do the work as well as you could—without needing outside assistance? If so, you will communicate your attitude to your employee, who will be reluctant to share even his legitimate questions, much less call for assistance from you. The result: He will be operating in fear, neither asking for nor receiving the support he needs. A person driven by fear will be reactive and anxious. And will produce inferior work. Your suspicions will seem justified—whereas in truth it was the suspicions themselves that created the unsatisfactory result.

Regardless of your history, you can enter the path to more trusting relationships at any point. The important thing is not where you are on the path—but that you are progressing.

If you take the risk, and your employee abuses your trust, see Tough Business Problem #60.

TOUGH BUSINESS PROBLEM #32

My subordinate failed. If I act with compassion and let her know I understand, what will motivate her to try harder next time?

The *I Ching* contends that man has received a nature that is innately good. Because this is true, it is worth taking the risk of believing that the individual in question has as much interest in rectifying and recovering from her failure—and in identifying the cause and avoiding a repetition—as you would if you found yourself in her situation.

Under these circumstances, correction and improvement become not a matter of punishment but of education. You promote those qualities in your associate that are constructive, such as her willingness to take a risk, her desire to learn from the situation, her eagerness to make amends. At the same time you diminish through compassion—rather than enlarge through punishment—those qualities that contributed to the failure.

You may be making a mistake in this case—perhaps her motivation and intent are not as unsullied as you want to believe. Even so, it is better to err from time to time by placing your trust in someone who proves unworthy of your empathy than to deny forever your willingness to take a leap of faith in order to honor the compassionate spirit within yourself.

There is no safety in honoring the compassion in your spirit. Life does not come with guarantees. Things will go wrong from time to time—for your subordinate as well as for you. Remember always, you cannot judge the health of your organization by the fact that it has problems. Every individual and every organization has problems.

Look, rather, to see whether you and your organization have a healthy process for addressing these problems—one that nurtures rather than damages spirit. You may be one of those fortunate individuals who have the opportunity both to help create and to experience a corporate culture that encourages people to bring their best—rather than their worst—to work with them every day.

If you do not believe that man has received a nature that is innately good, see Tough Business Problem #94.

TOUGH BUSINESS PROBLEM #33

I don't get the best thinking from my staff because they are trying too hard to please me by telling me what they think I want to hear. I've asked them to be more honest, but I'm frustrated by the fact that they are still holding back. What's wrong with them?

Although it may feel as though your staff is failing you, the truth is that this problem is not a symptom of failure on anybody's part—but rather a manifestation of your growth.

In the beginning, if you recall, you allowed yourself to be surrounded with people who were willing to give pleasing you precedence over expressing their authentic selves. You set the tone by responding defensively to feedback; you trained them to relate to you in the limited way that protected your sense of comfort, power, and security.

As it turns out, it was precisely these conditions that gave you a greenhouse environment in which you could send down roots strong enough to support new growth. Now you have outgrown the limited relationships that once served you. You are ready for more honesty from your staff, and you look to them to change their ways.

As noble as your intentions may be, you have presented an intimidating challenge to the status quo. It is scary to try out new behaviors in the workplace—especially behaviors having to do with taking risks, exposing oneself to criticism, allowing oneself to feel vulnerable and unprotected. Though you feel you are ready for the challenge of more honest relationships, you must understand that asking your staff to share the authentic expression of their inner selves with you comes at some cost to their personal sense of safety and security. And when you are making new demands upon your staff that require the development of inner qualities such as courage and faith, you cannot order these up from them on demand.

Do you have sufficient patience to suffer the discomfort that inevitably comes upon recognition of your desire for growth—while you are waiting for reality to catch up with your higher expectations?

The time it takes won't be wasted. For you still have work to do.

You have already grown into the recognition that you want more in your relationships. Now you must grow into someone worthy of having more in your relationships. In other words, in order to have employees who will trust you enough to take the kind of risk you are asking for, you will first have to demonstrate to them that you are trustworthy.

It is not just your staff who are being called upon to undertake new behaviors, but you as well. Some of these new behaviors will be:

- Sacrificing your option to summarily judge, criticize, and/or dismiss others' opinions, understanding that once you raise the stakes in a call for honest feelings and thoughts, you must be willing to take the time, energy, and self-discipline to give each a fair hearing
- Learning to give and receive negative feedback from a constructive rather than a defensive point of view
- Setting an inspiring role model for your staff by taking the risk of expressing your own real feelings and opinions to them

And perhaps the greatest challenge of all:

- Bringing compassion, humility, patience, and understanding to those who do not yet fully trust you

You may realize that becoming a trustworthy individual is a tall order. As tall an order in fact as the leap of faith you are asking your employees to take in you.

If you feel that every time you grow to a new level of development, things should go easier for you, and become frustrated when you discover that instead there's a whole other layer of challenges you never even knew about before; and if you hope that once you get past these *troubles, you'll have it handled once and for all, see Tough Business Problem #90.*

4

Life-Driven Leadership

The life of a man who has pu-
rified himself is a bright light for the people of the earth.

—The *I Ching*

TOUGH BUSINESS PROBLEM #34

In order to remain competitive, our company needs to pare its workforce dramatically. Upper management is talking about evaluating and ranking us against one another within each job category. The poorer performers will be let go. Isn't there a better way?

A company that is on the ropes needs to find the key to employee motivation—not demoralization. Formalizing competition within the corporate ranks as an across-the-board policy reads to the employees as well as the marketplace as a desperate act. Blame is being assigned for failure—and it is being laid upon those with the least amount of responsibility. This shortsighted approach may make perfect sense from a numbers point of view, but long-term it is likely to kill the company.

As long as corporate management views the marketplace as hostile, they will find no option other than to mirror this with the creation of an equally hostile internal environment. But this fear-driven reaction becomes a self-fulfilling prophecy. Pitting employees against each other in competition may achieve the kind of short-term productivity your company is looking for to stay afloat. Long-term it destroys whatever esprit de corps has been built up over the many years of the company's history.

Not only are the individuals who lose the competition demoralized, but those who hired them, worked with them, or reported to them are likewise negatively affected. This clearly communicates that management has lost faith in its viability . . . from the grassroots up. The harder they push the internal competition, the farther behind the company's ability to perform at increased expectations and standards will fall.

What your company has forgotten is that employees commit themselves to giving their best to their employers not when they are afraid of losing their jobs, but rather out of allegiance to the fundamental contribution to the community and corporate values the company represents. This allegiance has tangible benefit; it is even assigned monetary worth in the sale of a business under the category of "goodwill." This goodwill factor represents the positive feelings the company has built with its clientele and employees over the years.

To turn this culture around, top management must pry its focus from external, fear-generating factors and rekindle their vision sufficiently to rediscover, or if necessary re-create, a meaningful purpose for the company, one that makes a valid contribution to the community.

To begin this challenging process, the company must stop implying that it is the individual employee who has failed and instead begin to take responsibility for the fact that it is the company's commitment to its vision overall that has faltered. No one is scapegoated to carry the blame. Instead leadership is called to the task of identifying a use for corporate resources and assets that the marketplace will support. This will mean letting go of old systems and structures that no longer work and experimenting with new forms and formats for the company. As the corporation is released from its own history, it is freed to take on a new size and shape. This is a creative process, calling upon humanity's higher aspirations—qualities such as inspiration, vision, clarity, and service—rather than the lower aspirations—such as greed, fear, and selfishness, which are powerful but ultimately alienating forces induced by your company's proposed trash-and-slash program.

This life-driven approach does not mean that the company refrains from cutting staff—but not as an across-the-board policy based on fear. Yes, sacrifices will be called for. Choices must be made. Change is painful—and often messy. If you were to judge the butterfly in the midst of transformation by cutting open the caterpillar's cocoon, you would find only green mush. At times top management and employees alike will have little more than the memory of their original vision to hold on to.

But when management takes this leap, coming from faith rather than from fear, the company can be freed to evolve into the fullest expression of its potential. As the company evolves, so is each individual freed to fulfill his or her potential as well—either within or without the corporation. Faith is the key to employee motivation that transcends the vicissitudes of fate, and employee motivation holds the key to success in times of transition.

If you decide to take the risk of protesting the policy and find that as a result you've been given a poor-performance review, see Tough Business Problem #55.

If after many years you lose your job, see Tough Business Problem #97.

TOUGH BUSINESS PROBLEM #35

I believe the company I work for will pull through, but right now we are having financial difficulties. How can I keep my staff motivated when there's no hope of raises or bonuses?

Every man must follow something greater than himself—as the *I Ching* teaches "something that serves him as a lodestar."

To the degree that you share a vision with the company you work for that serves the greater community, to the degree that you have articulated this vision, and to the degree that you have sought and retained individuals who support this vision—this is the degree to which your team will hold together. Those who believe in what you are doing will stay motivated regardless of bonuses and raises.

When you have faith in your vision, your spirit shines like the sun, illuminating all within reach of its rays. But remember, the sun brings both good and bad into the light of day.

Are you really willing to see things as they are? For instance does your concern with material inducements indicate that your company's original vision has dimmed? Did the fame and fortune of the success of better times come to take its place, replacing the original vision of contributing to the community with the desire for material reward?

Have you become attached to your title, your position, the size of your team? Are you holding on tightly to your staff, not because they have become indispensable to your workload but because they have become indispensable to your ego? The *I Ching* warns that "only when a man is completely free from his ego, and intent upon what is right and essential, does he acquire the clarity that enables him to see through such people, and become free of blame."

Tough times bring out inner truths. To pierce through the illusions, you must find the courage to face the real question: not "How do I keep everyone motivated?'' but rather ''How do I find the strength to let those whose lodestar consists only of bonuses and raises go?''

Ironically, if you are willing to let go those who do not share the company's vision with you, regardless of the pain you may undergo as a result, you will in the end receive the greatest support. If you are among those individuals who are willing to renounce material rewards as the primary motivation for your work—you will in the end achieve the greatest success.

If you or your company has lost its vision, see Tough Business Problem #62.

If you're unable to keep your staff inspired, see Tough Business Problem #73.

TOUGH BUSINESS PROBLEM #36

I'm sure there's a lesson in here somewhere. Our company has some counterproductive policies that are undermining the morale of my team. By challenging these policies I'm getting a lot of flack from other groups in the company who liked things the way they were. What could I have done to avoid this?

In the name of "self-improvement," you are wasting valuable energy looking for the lesson in this.

I am reminded of a walk I once took through a nearby woods in order to restore my spirits. Feeling panicky as an important deadline approached, I courageously tore myself away from my work in order to revitalize and deepen my creative process. Just as I was beginning to feel my vitality returning, I felt the painful sting of a spider bite pounding the side of my face. I turned my fervent entreaty to God.

"God," I asked, "What did I do wrong? I courageously acted on my own behalf—I took a risk—I followed my heart. Why did I get bitten? Tell me. What is the lesson in this?"

The answer came back kindly but firmly.

"You humans. Your notion of your place in the universe is so grandiose. There was a lesson here indeed. But not for you. This one was for the spider."

How can you have greatness of spirit required of true leadership when you are so quick to see every situation as a "lesson" to you? Like someone peering through the crack of a door at life, your outlook is limited by your desire for self-improvement. When you become uncomfortable, you retreat from your convictions—seeing everything only as it relates to you and how you might have less pain next time. This blocks your view of the bigger picture.

Watch out for that part of you that wants to find out what went wrong so that you will never make that mistake again. Acting from your convictions is not a mistake. You would like to take your stand and then have everything turn out just the way you want. But life will spin out of your control sometimes. You will never be good enough, diligent enough, smart enough, lucky enough, or spiritual enough to get it to turn out the way you want each and every time. You must be big enough now to do what is in your heart to do—and be willing to take the consequences.

To be a leader, you must rise above your self-indulgent urge for the illusion of control to find the requisite strength to serve as a central figure around whom other persons may unite. You must be willing to face your destiny and take the consequences.

If you think having to take consequences is unfair, see Tough Business Problem #52.

TOUGH BUSINESS PROBLEM #37

I was just about to fire a relatively new employee who has proven to be incompetent, when her mother unexpectedly died. She's taking a week off for the funeral and to handle family affairs. The business can't afford to keep her on— but how and when do I let her go? Can I do it while she's gone so she can spend more time at home—and to save us the money? Or should I wait until she returns?

You already know your timing is unfortunate. Had you fired her before her loss, you'd be off the hook. But you didn't.

Now it's a whole new ball game. Here's why. This new, incompetent employee may well have been little more than an unfortunate inconvenience to you before the death in her family . . . a drain on your cash flow that you are eager to resolve. But she stands before you now, reeling from her loss, as a reminder of the great tragedy of the human condition—the inevitability of our own mortality. Regardless of how new or how incompetent she is, at the moment that she suffers a loss, she becomes the Universal Employee. Now upon the heels of her mother's death, the last thing she needs is to have to deal with the shock of being fired and the necessity of looking for new work.

But it's equally important to understand that this crisis is not just about her. Every person on your staff will be looking to you to see how you handle this situation. If you are generous and kind, your staff will understand that in a crisis you will be there for them as well.

So what should you do? Don't fire her while she's home in mourning. Don't even fire her upon her return. Accommodate her tragedy by allowing her to return from her absence and work for a sufficient period of time to regain some degree of stability in her life. Two months should be an adequate period of time. Then, following stan-

169

dard firing procedures for your company, if she is still incompetent, go ahead and give her notice.

But you say you can't afford to keep a nonfunctioning salary on your books? Think again. If you are in business, you've got to be prepared for the fact that natural disasters may affect your financial well-being from time to time. Whether from something as out of your control as an earthquake taking out your telephone lines, a riot shutting down your operation, or the death of the mother of a new, incompetent employee, your business is bound to be severely challenged from time to time.

If your finances are so tenuous that two months' salary to one employee can take you under, you might as well deal with the real issue—the viability of your company—sooner rather than later. You can thrash about bemoaning your fate—blaming yourself, the employee, or mortality itself—or you can gracefully adapt yourself to the conditions of the time.

Most likely, if you follow this advice, you will survive the loss of two months' salary. You will be taking a financial hit, but your remaining staff will repay you many times over with their reignited loyalty and respect. A team who trusts that their leader will not desert them when confronted by the vicissitudes of fate will take its strength from the very roots of the human experience.

If you'd like to follow this advice but your business could go under if you do, see Tough Business Problem #49.

If you already fired her, see Tough Business Problem #76.

TOUGH BUSINESS PROBLEM #38

I spent years putting together a loyal and committed team of employees. Now the economic downturn has decimated our earnings with no break in sight. I've made every other cut I can. Should I borrow to tide us over until business improves or resort to cutting staff, knowing that it will destroy the morale of those who remain?

You speak of morale, but are you really contributing to your company's morale by attempting to close the gap between reality and illusion at the expense of your own ability to take decisive action? Do you really think so little of your "loyal and committed staff" that you expect them to keep their spirits high while watching you dance on burning coals? Is it trust in the universe to detour around your pain through the use of smoke and mirrors—borrowing here, stretching payments there, massaging your tax returns, exploiting years of good faith to enroll the bank as a partner in your avoidance?

Rather, the *I Ching* teaches the superior man to meet fate with an attitude of acceptance. When fate summons you, you must be willing to surrender everything to the bonfire of truth. What you need now is a firm grasp on reality—a willingness to act quickly and decisively to realign your expenditures with your income. You will not be able to do so until you become willing to take on the pain in this.

The years you spent putting together your cherished team, the individuals who came to work for the good of the company and who must now be asked to leave for the very same reason—that is the sacrifice that is called for. That is the leap of faith that you must be willing to make.

You must not use your spirituality to avoid your pain. "The superior man learns from the situation what is demanded of him and then follows this intimation from fate."

If you are worried about the morale of your staff because there is no hope of bonuses or raises for those who remain even after painful layoffs, see Tough Business Problem #35.

TOUGH BUSINESS PROBLEM #39

One candidate for the critical position we need to fill has average ability—but an extraordinary commitment to putting all that he has to use on behalf of this company. The other candidate is superior at what the job calls for— with an extraordinary commitment to advancing his own career. Which would be the better hire?

The issue at the heart of this dilemma is What does it take to succeed in business? Skills, brilliance, talent—of course these things are important. But they mean little if they are not put to use in service of something greater than gratifying one's own ego.

Businesses are living organizations, composed of people who have come together for a common purpose. The *I Ching* teaches that "true fellowship among men must be based upon a concern that is universal. It is not the private interests of the individual that create lasting fellowship among men, but rather the goals of humanity."

Let someone who is watching out only for himself into your organization, believing you can channel his energy to serve your own ends, and you will soon discover that when the superstar has tasted power, he will want to begin calling the shots. Because the success that has come to your company as a result of his efforts have attached itself to him, not to you, your desire to preserve the now-inflated status quo will seem to lend his point of view credence. Meanwhile, by taking this superstar as your shortcut to success and compromising your own vision as well as the morale of your organization overall, whatever potential your less-promising staff could have realized will have atrophied in the interim.

From your perspective the self-interested superstar may seem manageable enough at first. But the *I Ching* teaches that "a pig that is still young and lean cannot rage around much, but after it has eaten

173

its fill and become strong, its true nature comes out. . . . "

You are wise to stop and admit the whole truth to yourself about your candidates while you can still do something about it, rather than greedily gobbling the one whose superior skills promise the quickest return. When forced to choose, select spirit over talent. But better yet, hold out for someone who has both superior skill and commitment to your vision.

If it's too late—and the superstar has already left you reeling in his wake—see Tough Business Problem #56.

TOUGH BUSINESS PROBLEM #40

I can think of a number of people in my company who could be a lot better off if only they'd go into therapy. How should I broach this subject?

The best way to encourage people to seek out therapeutic resources is to be a healthy role model yourself.

Before you broach the subject of their seeking out therapy with anyone, take this little quiz, to see how you rate:

TRUE OR FALSE

1. I am patient with other people's problems, willing to lend a sympathetic ear without needing to fix or change them or their situation in any way.
   True_____ False_____

2. I know how to protect myself and my space so that other people's problems do not impose themselves on my time or energy any more than I am freely willing to give.
   True_____ False_____

3. I understand that happiness is not necessarily a prerequisite for mental health. People have the right to be fully alive, and that includes times of pain and suffering as well as times of joy and serenity.
   True_____ False_____

4. I am humble and reverent in relation to other people's pacing and processes, admitting that I am not adequate to the task of judging another's internal experiences.
   True_____ False_____

5. My urge to reach out to others comes with no strings attached. I have no ulterior motive, agenda, or purpose other than to be of service to that individual.
   True_____ False_____

6. I know myself well enough to be certain that my desire to help others does not come as a diversion to taking the far greater risk of telling the truth and courageously addressing my own weaknesses and needs.
   True_____ False_____

7. I believe that the universe's support and guidance is as readily available for these others in their own lives as it is in my own. I can rest assured that they are progressing on their own journeys to mental health and fulfillment via the most direct route, without my needing to do anything about it.
   True_____ False_____

When your response to every one of these seven questions is *true*, you will have the answer to your sticky business problem. You will not be needing to broach the subject of therapy with anyone. When someone needs help, he or she willingly comes to you for guidance.

If you did poorly on this quiz and think maybe you could use a little therapy yourself, see Tough Business Problem #92.

TOUGH BUSINESS PROBLEM #41

Who should pick up the lunch tab?

OLD PARADIGM: Whoever most wants the other to be in his debt.
NEW PARADIGM: Whoever is moved to give to another with no strings attached, knowing that what is given in the right spirit will come back to him from the primal depths of the universe many times multiplied, sometime, some way.

If you think the new paradigm is hogwash, see Tough Business Problem #94.

5

Risk Taking

To be circumspect and not to forget one's armor is the right way to security.

—The *I Ching*

TOUGH BUSINESS PROBLEM #42

I took a risk. Things aren't going as well as I would have hoped by now, but I still believe in my idea. My family and friends are begging me to give up. Should I?

Moments come in every life where shock comes upon shock, that which the *I Ching* calls "thunder repeated."

At such moments the superior man recognizes that he is being called to set his life in order and search his heart "lest it harbor any secret opposition to the will of God."

This invocation will help you achieve the attitude of the superior man, who, even when standing alone in an apparently hostile world, has faith that "if he will only see to it that he is possessed of something truly spiritual, the time is bound to come, sooner or later, when the difficulties will be resolved and all will go well."

INVOCATION FOR ONE WHO STANDS ALONE

May I find the courage to follow the dictates of my heart wherever they may lead, understanding that my heart is wise and caring enough to take into consideration the loving advice of my family and friends, honest enough to help me differentiate those tasks that are worth risking one's life for—from those that are not.

If by following diligently, I find myself standing alone, may I stand like a tree on a hillside
Visible from afar
Undaunted, patient, serene
Preparing myself for my moment to arrive:
The opportunity to provide shade to all those who come to seek shelter beneath my boughs.

If serenity continues to elude you in your solitude, see Tough Business Problem #49.

TOUGH BUSINESS PROBLEM #43

I keep going back and forth on this one. The company I own and run is doing fine right now, but long-term I've got a problem I can't seem to get a grip on. If I don't invest in new equipment for my company, the industry may leave us behind. If I do, it could take that much more than we've got short-term to break even. What should I do?

You think your insecurity and confusion are a liability. Furthermore you think you need to be certain you are making the right decision before you act.

But Confucius says: ·

Danger arises when a man feels secure in his position.
Destruction threatens when a man seeks to preserve his worldly estate.
Confusion develops when a man has put everything in order.

Therefore the superior man does not forget danger in his security,
Nor ruin when he is well established,
Nor confusion when his affairs are in order.
In this way he gains personal safety and is able to protect the empire.

Your fear and restlessness indicate that you are in full possession of your powers. Take comfort in the fact that your insecurity and disorder provide such fertile ground for growth, keeping you on your toes. Now what is most important is to make full use of the time.

In fact the only thing that will cause certain harm to your company is your continuing to hold out for guarantees that you will make the right decision, your preference for having perfect clarity and faith in place before you act.

Baron Wen Chi a contempory of Confucius, said that he always thought three times before he acted. When Confucius heard this, he remarked, "To think twice is quite enough."

If you're putting off this decision until you're absolutely certain what to do, see Tough Business Problem #49.

If you make the wrong decision, see Tough Business Problem #53.

TOUGH BUSINESS PROBLEM #44

I hate my job—but I know I'm lucky to have it. In this economy do I risk trying to make a change to something I could feel passionate about, or should I hang in there until the economy improves?

Enlightenment occurs the moment you stop pulling fearfully at the reigns of control and surrender to your life, the universe—even the economy—exactly as it is. When you can do this, you loosen your grip on your desire, with the understanding that faith is disorderly. You cannot know what is going to happen to you, not even one moment from now. When you least expect it, new directions will make themselves known to you—adventures! surprises!

If you are not in such a place of surrender now, you must learn to give your current situation the best that you can under the circumstances—all the while having patience and faith that you are advancing toward a future greater than anything you have yet imagined for yourself.

You don't have to feel passionate about your job to feel passionate about your life. Enthusiasm is catching. Let it begin anywhere, and watch with amazement as even the most resistant timber catches fire.

Where to begin? Sing in the bathtub. Tap-dance while the computer prints out. Treat yourself to the rarest cheese on the shelf. Take every opportunity to jump out of yourself and into humor, openness, perspective, and faith.

When your passion is reignited, follow it wherever it may lead. If you are not ready to hand in your resignation and leap into a void, you can—at least—take a class on the subject, or maybe an after-hours internship, join the professional association, or be on the lookout for a mentor.

Use your very life as fuel, and trust that while the fire in your heart is transforming your inner experience, the heat and warmth you are producing will be attracting new opportunities to you beyond your wildest dreams.

If you decide to stay in your job, but transform your experience of it, see Tough Business Problem #59.

If you'd like to take the leap to find something better, but you can't muster sufficient passion to push through your fear, see Tough Business Problem #12.

TOUGH BUSINESS PROBLEM #45

I've got six years to go until retirement with full benefits, but I hate every day I spend on the job. Should I quit and risk going for a job that I will enjoy more—or keep hanging on?

If your intention is to live well and fully in retirement, then know this: Living well takes practice. You are teaching yourself about life every moment of every day. Who you will be six years from now has everything to do with the decisions you make today.

So I ask you, when you reach retirement, who will it be who collects the benefits? Is it the fully alive person you fantasize—or someone who has trained himself year after year to deny his spirit?

The *I Ching* teaches that "If we are in pursuit of game and want to get a shot at a quarry, we must set about it in the right way. A man who persists in stalking game in a place where there is none may wait forever without finding any. Persistence in search is not enough. What is not sought in the right way is not found."

If you know that staying in this job is a living death, but your spouse is urging you to hang in for the sake of security, see Tough Business Problem #42.

If you'd like to leap, but something's holding you back, see Sticky Business Problem #12.

If you realize that to begin to search for fulfillment the right way, you will need to begin by looking at why and how you got into a position that you hate so much in the first place, see Tough Business Problem #59.

TOUGH BUSINESS PROBLEM #46

The whole family has sacrificed a lot over the years to keep the family business going. Part of me sees how I could take over the business and grow it into something much bigger, and part of me feels that's the last thing in the world I'd want to do. How can I handle my fear?

When considering the possibility of expanding the family business, do you, in addition to feeling fear, feel inspiration?

Or do you just feel scared?

Fear coupled with inspiration is success's most powerful ally, the source of motivation, excitement, dynamic tension—the creative edge. Do you feel scared *and* inspired about expanding the business?

On the other hand, fear alone is insufficient motivation upon which to base future success. This includes such fear-based derivatives as guilt, shame, pity, and the desire for approval from others—qualities that may well be fueling your urge to strong-arm your way through your resistance. There is danger inherent in relying entirely on one's own power, in pushing ahead regardless of whether or not what you are doing is the right thing for you at that time.

"Truly great power does not degenerate into mere force but remains inwardly united with the fundamental principles of right and of justice," says the *I Ching*.

What is justice? To be "just" is traditionally interpreted as being fair to others. In your case you are grateful for what your family has given you, and, you feel that it is fair and right to give back to them. But there is another interpretation of justice that you must now consider. It is this: You must apply this virtue not only to others, but to yourself. You must be fair with yourself.

Now is the time to ask and answer the tough questions. How often have you sacrificed your own needs to serve the family business already? How often have you quelled divergent desires in order to keep things going? How much of what you are about to do is about pleasing others, and how much about responding to your inner imperative to act on your own behalf? Are you being fair to yourself?

If you were to cut yourself some slack—the kind of justice you easily extend to your family but find so difficult to make available to yourself—you might realize that the heavy emotion you experience around this issue genuinely deserves and warrants your taking sufficient time to figure out what you really want for yourself.

This is a whole other level of endeavor than you've brought to bear against your goals in the past. Instead of single-mindedly pushing yourself to succeed *despite yourself*, you are now being guided to look for the way to expand toward a greater experience of success that *includes yourself.*

Before you can know what's right for you to do, you must take your fear seriously. On the one hand, your fear may be a healthy indication that you are on exactly the right track. The person who feels no fear in her life is probably not taking enough risks. In this case, expanding the family business may well be a risk worth taking.

On the other hand, your fear may be a vital warning that you are swimming against the current of your own life purpose. This growing realization may be coupled with the understandable fear you feel in telling your family that you are going to follow your heart in a direction that does not include them.

When you can face up to your fear, be it through taking the risk of expanding the family business, or by declaring to your family that your destiny in life lies elsewhere, you will be experiencing true power. While you will still feel fear, you will no longer be scared to death—but to life.

If you decide it is your destiny to stay and build the business, recognizing that you are being scared to life, see Tough Business Problem #15.

If you realize it's time to move on, but you're afraid to face your boss, who also happens to be your father, see Tough Business Problem #4.

If you leave and as a result get disowned, see Tough Business Problem #60.

TOUGH BUSINESS PROBLEM #47

I've been meaning to ask you this question for quite a while, but I couldn't find the right words. The bottom line is that I procrastinate. What can I do about this affliction?

Procrastination is perfectionism. Ask yourself about the voice that says you won't do it good enough.

If you wish your ordinary self were enough, see Tough Business Problem #90.

TOUGH BUSINESS PROBLEM #48

I need help right now! I've been called to come to my boss's office immediately and I have no idea why. How can I make it all the way there without flipping out?

You have to take that lonely walk to your boss's office. You can take that walk in fear and trepidation—quivering in fear and anticipation, dredging up memories of long-buried shortcomings, and working up fervent defenses for each one—thereby ensuring that the individual who arrives at his boss's doorway at the conclusion of that walk is in the worst possible shape. Or there's an alternative: You can take that walk in such a way that you arrive vital and alert, ready for anything—bad news or good!

It is in your own best interest to arrive in the latter state, since bosses, like dogs, can catch the scent of panic exuded by even the most devoted employee. And even if your boss's original intention was something as innocent as coordinating trip schedules, remember: The boss who sniffs panic suspects guilt. If you are defensive, he'll wonder what you're hiding.

Let the scent of confidence waft through the room, on the other hand, and your boss might find himself wondering why you haven't been tapped for a raise or a promotion lately.

Here's how to take that long walk on neutralizing ground, each added step transforming your anxiety to confidence. It may sound easier than it is to actually pull this off. It may require practice. But given the number of times you will be called to take long, lonely walks in your life—be it to the boss's office, to a dissatisfied customer's conference room, or to the dentist's chair—you will have plenty of opportunity.

So you've been summoned. Sit quietly for a moment. Close your eyes. And take several deep breaths. If your heart is pounding, continue breathing slowly until you begin to get a handle on your anxiety.

Good. Now gently lift yourself from your seat. Let the bottoms of your shoes make contact with the earth. Can you feel the floor pressing against your feet? Move your right foot. Left foot. Feel the connection between your feet and the earth below.

Keep moving, timing your deep breathing to each step. Right foot—breathe in; left foot—out; right foot—in; left foot—out. Keep your mind and your attention on the connection between ground and foot and your slow, easy breathing. If a fear or concern breaks into your thinking, lightly acknowledge it, then let it go by returning your attention to the physical sensations of walking and breathing.

When you approach his door, take one final deep breath to release any of the last bits of fear or tension and, thus emptied, present yourself with neutral anticipation.

Chances are the summons was good news. But in even the worst-case scenario you will at least have the peace of mind that you have brought your best rather than worst possible self to handle whatever fate brings your way.

If you consistently expect the worst to happen, see Tough Business Problem #99.

If you consistently expect the worst to happen because you know, in your heart of hearts, that you've done something wrong, see Tough Business Problem #64.

If the worst does happen, see Tough Business Problem #100.

TOUGH BUSINESS PROBLEM #49

I have a critical decision I need to make now. No matter how much information I gather, how keenly I tune in to my heart, how much help I seek out, I'm still unclear about the right thing to do. What can I do to ensure that I don't make the wrong choice?

Rebecca, a creative child, felt inspired to build a raft to float down the river that meandered through her village. Instinctively she constructed a raft that would take any waves or eddies the river brought her way. She placed the raft in the river, tied securely to the shore. She longed for her adventure to begin, putting her craft to the test. But being as cautious as she was clever, she sought the advice of the other villagers before launching her handmade craft.

She went first to the village parson, who, fearing that Rebecca's raft might careen into the banks of the river, instructed her to add a rudder. This Rebecca did, grateful that she had such a wise and caring adviser.

Then she went to the village blacksmith, who, fearing that Rebecca would have no way to stop her raft, forged and donated to her a great anchor made of iron. Rebecca accepted this gift, relieved that the blacksmith had remembered what she had so foolishly forgotten.

Then she went to her relatives, who fearing her slight size, gave her sacks of sand for extra ballast.

At last she was ready. The villagers gathered on the shore as she untied the raft and started her adventure downstream. But just as she loosened the reins, a friend arrived with one last gift: a life preserver.

''Throw it to me!'' Rebecca shouted. The crowd watched as the weight of the canvas ring, on top of all of their well-meaning contributions, proved to be too much for the raft, which promptly sank.

As Rebecca swam safely to shore, she realized that it was in truth her fears that had swamped the raft. Rebecca did have a great adventure—and while she preferred that it had been that of taking her hand-built raft downstream—the adventure of seeing the truth about the price of her urge for safety was at the moment the far greater gift. Not only did she soon successfully build and launch a raft along the lines of her original vision but she learned the secret to tackling destiny head-on.

Here is an invocation for the Rebecca in you:

INVOCATION FOR RISK TAKERS

May I acknowledge myself for carefully considering the beginning, resisting the urge to come to quick, superficial resolution in order to send my roots into this issue deep and firm.

Now that it is time to act, I have the foundation upon which to take a courageous stand. Even if clarity and certainty yet elude me, I am willing to tackle my destiny head-on, remembering that if there were not the potential for pain as a result of making a choice, it would not be a risk. Where there is no risk, there can be no growth.

I make my best decision—given the information and intuition I have available to me at this time—willing to take the consequences whatever they may be. I find comfort in the knowledge that I am fully able and willing to respond and self-correct, should that be necessary.

May I come to trust that responding to the entreaties of my heart with my best guess is always good enough. And that on the only path that truly counts—the path to increased wisdom, love, and knowledge—there are, in truth, no dead ends.

TOUGH BUSINESS PROBLEM #50

I dream of starting a company coaching people to take risks—but I'm afraid I'll fail. What am I missing?

How can you give to others what you don't have?

If you feel you would like to push through your fear, see Tough Business Problem #12.

6

Failure and Crisis

As long as a man's inner nature remains stronger and richer than anything offered by external fortune, as long as he remains inwardly superior to fate, fortune will not desert him.

—The *I Ching*

TOUGH BUSINESS PROBLEM #51

What do I do when I'm informed I'm being audited by the IRS?

It can be a shock when something forces you to confront the fact that there is a reality external to yourself and your life that you cannot control. Being chosen at random for an audit by a computer thousands of miles away is one of those occasions. It can be an even bigger occasion if you suspect that you have done something that may have somehow contributed to getting selected. Your first response is likely to be one of resistance: "Life is unfair," you may say. Or you may ask, "Why me—poor me?" "What will become of me?" or "Why am I being punished?"

These emotions are burden enough. But in the case of the individual with spiritual aspirations it is tempting to load up on additional tonnage by feeling bad about feeling bad: "Where is my faith when I need it? I can't even have faith right."

You not only have resistance to the audit, you have resistance to your resistance. So, the first thing to do when being informed you are being audited by the IRS is *stop resisting*. Surrender.

Where do you begin?

Step One: First let yourself feel all of your feelings. Set aside a prescribed period of time to wallow fully. Following a life-driven philosophy does not mean that you should or even can avoid feeling fear or anger. While you aspire to a quiet heart, there are no shortcuts around or through negative feelings when they have a legitimate cause.

In fact, when faced with the unknown—be it a growling animal or an accountant wielding a pen with red ink—a short-term burst of fear or anger can be a lifesaver. Adrenaline can sharpen your senses, spur you to action, summon forth your primal survival instincts.

196

Even crisis-induced shame and guilt has its purpose, forcing to the light of day those issues you have managed to avoid confronting—perhaps for some time.

But before turning your angst into a career, a dose of perspective is in order. An IRS audit is not something that has happened to you alone. It has happened to many, many individuals—the vast majority of whom have survived the experience. Believe it or not, some have even emerged better, happier people as a result. The remaining steps will show you how to put your survival instincts to work to help make your IRS audit a potentially life-affirming experience. (Yes, this *is* possible.)

Step Two: You've learned that you are at your best when you are calm and confident. Certainly this is the desirable state for your audit. You're not there yet? Then delegate stability to a qualified accountant who does not share your fear of the unknown in this situation. Top candidate: someone who actually worked on the other side of the fence as an IRS auditor. Get someone smart and supportive who you believe will do everything within his or her professional power to get you the best possible outcome. Then follow his or her direction and advice with full cooperation.

There are plenty of former agents for hire. They talk the language, know the systems, may even be familiar with the individuals assigned to your case. Remember, for the agent—and your own CPA—your audit is not about life and death; it's about nine to five. Yes, as grand as this occasion is for you, it's just another day's work for just about everybody else involved. Deflating, isn't it? But it is also a spiritual boon, preparing the way for you to take the next step.

Step Three: Accept your imperfection. The *I Ching* teaches us that it is the law of heaven to make fullness empty and to make full what is modest. During a year's period of transactions there are bound to be discrepancies, flukes, and flaws—some omissions and some commissions in your records that will need to be addressed. You are, after all, human. Things happen.

If you take an aggressive stance, getting sidetracked by the defense of what you contend to be your impeccable reputation, record-keeping ability, and pious intentions, you will complicate the transaction needlessly. If, on the other hand, you are willing to honor your human limitations, your unassuming attitude will provide maximum opportunity for your team members—your accountant and your IRS agent—to attend to the task at hand quickly and simply. The *I Ching* teaches, ''Where no claims are put forward, no resistances arise.''

Step Four: through modesty you have created the environment within which the best possible outcome is most likely to transpire. This is an extremely valuable skill, which you can use in any future negotiations. You have also faced what may well be among your worst fears, turning potential crisis into a manageable process. If you can do this with an audit, you can face any circumstance life may present to you. This is a priceless gift—the gift of liberation from fear. But for you, it will cost only whatever dollar amount your tax team has worked out for you to pay. Such a deal!

Step Five: With equal parts of relief and gratitude you write the check to the IRS. This is no ordinary bill-paying session. This is the ritual completion of the sacrifice of your fear and arrogance. You are, as a result of your audit, at a new level of empowerment. The audit is over—and now anything is possible.

If you create the optimum environment for the best possible results to transpire—and you don't like what the best possible results are—see Tough Business Problem #100.

If your accountant begs you to keep better records next time, but you feel that someone with your talents, responsibilities, and spiritual depth is above such mundane considerations, see Tough Business Problem #52.

TOUGH BUSINESS PROBLEM #52

What words of wisdom do you have for the person who thinks you can have it all?

Business is tough, and you can't always do something about it.

TOUGH BUSINESS PROBLEM #53

What do I do when for some reason beyond my control the bottom falls out of the market or my product line becomes obsolete? What if disaster strikes? An earthquake? A war?

When I was very young, I took refuge in the belief that if I was good enough, worked hard enough, prayed, meditated, and loved enough, nothing bad would ever happen to me. As I grew over the years, I found solace in knowing that while bad things could happen to me, I had sufficient inner resources to overcome anything that might come my way—all the time struggling to keep my comfort level sufficiently high so as not to have to put my faith truly to the test. As time wore on, I became increasingly desperate in my attempts to avoid facing my secret demon: my fear that when finally summoned, my selfless love and spirituality would falter.

During World War II my father faced such a test just after passing his exams to be a physician. He was thrown into battle as a doctor in the Philippines. Under extremely adverse circumstances he tended to soldiers struggling with their injuries and illnesses. He did the best he could until he himself succumbed to a tropical fever. He lay shivering on a cot in the medic's tent, dehydrated and delirious.

As his fever peaked, orders arrived from headquarters that his battalion was to evacuate their position immediately. In the panic that ensued, the tent was disassembled, the troops boarded and moved out. When my father's consciousness broke through the sweat and delirium, he found that he had accidentally been left behind—one deathly ill young man on a lonely cot in the middle of a barren field.

Laughing.

Perhaps it was the fever, perhaps it was something more than that, but when my father realized what had happened to him, he instinctively knew he had to make a choice. He could resist his fate, spending his final reserves of energy flailing against the unfairness of it all, or he could give himself willingly to it and live. As my father tells it, he remembers laughing a long, long time. In fact he was still laughing when his fellow medics returned to retrieve him, dodging bullets as they carried him back to the safety of their new camp.

This was not a laughter that trivialized suffering. This was the laughter of one who had willingly fed himself to his demons and emerged triumphant. His laughter chimed through the remainder of World War II and down through the years as my legacy of spirit triumphant—of life emerging from the darkness, fear, and anger—to proclaim again and again and yet again, "I am willing."

Over seventy years ago, the English writer and critic Katherine Mansfield wrote in her journal, "There is no limit to human suffering. When one thinks 'Now I have touched the bottom of the sea—now I can go no deeper,' one goes deeper. And so it is for ever. . . . "

"I do not want to die without leaving a record of my belief that suffering can be overcome. For I do believe it. What must one do? There is no question of what is called 'passing beyond it.' This is false.

"One must submit. Do not resist. Take it. Be overwhelmed. Accept it fully. Make it part of life."

When put to the test in my own life, there is only one question to be answered: Am I willing? Am I willing when fate has taken away my last refuge—when there is no place to hide?

I aspire to be a selfless person who has faith in life no matter what, but at moments like these, so painfully exposed, devoid of the comforting illusions of the status quo to cushion and protect me, often all I can say is that I don't really know the whole truth about me—and I fear the worst. But out of this very act of acceptance, I, too, make my choice.

"The present agony will pass—if it doesn't kill," writes Mansfield. "If I can cease reliving all the shock and horror of it, cease going over it, I will get stronger."

INVOCATION FOR BAD TIMES

When the sun arrives at its new dawn, it turns toward its setting.
The moon when it is full begins to wane.
The flowering plant grows toward the sun, and from the weight of
its own blossom bends to the ground and dies.

This heavenly law works itself out in the fate of man also. Knowing
that he is helpless before the law of heaven, the superior man relin-
quishes the illusion of control, willing to surrender everything he has
to the conditions of the time.

Even the cherished notion of his faith and selflessness, weighing
him down like a heavy sack clutched in his grip.

He can not take another step, burdened as he is. To continue to
hold it tight in a fist of fear is certain death. In such a time, he has
no recourse but to tear the sack open and throw the seeds of his life
to the wind
releasing,
surrendering,
crying for mercy,
feeling the pain.

If he is blessed with willingness, he can watch many seeds blow
away, rejoicing for even the one that lands at his feet in the fertile
soil enriched by fallen flowers long past.

It will take root.

He may yet feel the urgency of resolution pressing hard upon him
but he must not pull at the seed, forcing it to emerge from the nurturing soil before its time.

Rather, he tends the bare, dark spot of earth diligently
with patience and discipline,

watering and weeding,
waiting and watching,
force of habit keeping order through the long winter.

Thus is the law of heaven that when the sun is at its zenith it rises toward a new dawn.
The moon when empty of light waxes again.

Through the dark patch of fertile soil, a seed sends up a tender, green shoot.

Can you find it in your heart to be willing to accept it all?

TOUGH BUSINESS PROBLEM #54

My whole life seems to be one of those occasions to which I must rise. When I don't have the option of taking time away to recuperate, how can I keep myself vital and energetic?

I once received a lesson from a Zen teacher that I would like to share with you. She was among the most tireless of all the teachers at her retreat center, able to wake even before the predawn rising bell. All day she divided her time between her many duties, moving gracefully from studying and teaching to more mundane tasks, such as making salad, sweeping floors. Even the younger residents looked up to her in awe.

"What is your secret?" I asked.

She explained that most people see their lives as divided into a concentrated period for work, followed by an isolated period of rest, followed by another period of work, and so on. She, on the other hand, chose to weave the two together in an elegant tapestry of give-and-take. Finely attuned to her inner world, it is her habit to give her work everything she has, paying special attention to the moment she has learned to recognize that comes just before her energy is about to give out. At that moment she takes a mental, physical, and spiritual break for as long as she needs to rejuvenate.

The break she takes gives her the opportunity to clear out leftover debris from the passing time—old worries that never amounted to anything, situations now past that have already been addressed, and thoughts for the future as well—hopes and fears. In fact she takes the occasion of her breaks to give all of her personal support systems a well-deserved rest, allowing them to revitalize and refuel. Thus rested, she said, clarity and energy return on their own—and she is renewed and refreshed.

But I had never seen her stop her work and take such a break. Mystified, I pressed her for an explanation.

She responded by teaching me the "half-smile meditation." In this rejuvenating technique you begin by placing a small smile on your face—not so big that if you looked in a mirror, you would see that you were smiling, but big enough that you can feel the muscles at either side of your mouth turn its corners up. Keeping your eyes open, you then breathe in and out a minimum of three times. You can do this meditation for as many breaths as it takes to regain your energy.

While you are taking your breaths, you clear your mind to think of nothing but the physical sensations of the upturned corners of your mouth and the slow, gentle breaths. If a thought comes into your mind, you acknowledge it and let it go by bringing your thoughts back to your physical sensations.

In this way you clear your mind, your emotions, your spirit, and your physical body, allowing them to rest empty for the moment or moments before your energy returns.

The beauty of this meditation—and the Zen teacher's secret—is that you can do this while making the transition from one task to another, as you perform routine physical work such as washing dishes or stuffing envelopes, even while sitting in a meeting or before a group. In fact it can become a wonderful challenge to find and use those many moments that so often drain us—as we stand in a long line, are stuck in traffic, or must sit through a boring lecture—by turning them into private half-smile retreats.

By giving yourself periodic—or even dozens—of these breaks throughout the day, you will easily find yourself able to meet whatever challenges come your way with both the necessary energy and the clarity that success requires.

If you look in the mirror and see that you are sneering instead of smiling, see Tough Business Problem #94.

TOUGH BUSINESS PROBLEM #55

I brought my best to the situation at hand—but failed anyway. What's to be done now?

The *I Ching* teaches us that difficulties throw a man back upon himself. The inferior man bewails his fate, thrashing about in self-pity and despair. The superior man views the obstruction as an occasion for inner enrichment.

Can you be this generous with yourself? This invocation is rich soil in which to plant the seed of recovery.

INVOCATION FOR ONE WHO HAS FAILED

I am where I am and it's all right.

The goal I sought represents a commitment to a process, including success and failure along the way.

When I fail, I replace judgment with observation.

I trust myself to correct what I can. Forgive myself for what I can't.

My worthiness does not depend on my achievements or the things that happen to me.

My worthiness is not up for question.

Knowing that there is more that I want for myself does not invalidate what I already have.

Regardless of how much at a standstill I feel myself to be right now, the currents of my destiny continue to work on my behalf, moving me forward to an even greater future than I have yet envisioned.

TOUGH BUSINESS PROBLEM #56

I gave my trusted associate tremendous responsibility, helping him build his reputation in our field. Then suddenly, without warning, he left our firm to set up a competitive company. Where did I go wrong?

When you've been burned in the business arena, often the initial response is to say, "It was wrong to put my trust in someone. I won't make that mistake again."

But putting faith in others is *not* a mistake. This is not to say that your gut instincts about others will always be correct and that you will not be hurt again. The greatest con artists can come in the loveliest guises—a talented young man who reminds you of yourself when you were young, for instance, or the devoted assistant who would do anything for you, year after year.

While some are aware of their exploitive and dishonest strategies, others are not conscious of their own darker potential. Denying it to themselves, they are totally capable of slipping past your duplicity-radar systems to wreak all manner of damage to your workplace, not to mention your psyche.

But should you mistakenly put your trust in such a person, there is some very good news. The *I Ching* teaches us that this is danger that comes to you from outside yourself. While it is painful, danger that comes from outside cannot get a firm foothold in your life. It will soon pass on and out.

This is not to say that you don't go back over your history with your assailant, looking for warning signs and signals you may have overlooked. Certainly you can always find something in which you erred. You can and should learn from the things that happen to you.

But you must take special care at this juncture not to pile mistake upon mistake, believing that the real lesson here is to refrain in the future from taking the risk of putting trust in others. In your work life you must often take such leaps of faith—knowing that pain may come as a result. You must heed your urge to mentor others, to share responsibility, to ask for help, to give others the gift of your friendship and support, to help others fulfill their potential.

If you choose the alternative, opting to play it safe, you deny the passionate entreaties of your life force beckoning you to expand. This is a danger from within—containing the potential to cause you far more damage in the long run than anything this assistant or anybody else could do to you. You might lose income because of the deeds of another, but only you can harm your most precious asset: your own spirit.

Even with all this understanding you bring to it, you will feel pain. Where did you go wrong? Feeling pain is not necessarily a symptom that you've made a mistake. This pain has great value for you. It is the caldron of the chaos of illusions pierced, of the burning away of the old and outgrown, of making space for the possibility of new creation.

If it still really burns you that people with flawed integrity can have successful careers, see Tough Business Problem #63.

If you are the associate and you can't imagine how it would be possible for someone to pursue his own ambitions without hurting his boss or mentor, see Tough Business Problem #4.

TOUGH BUSINESS PROBLEM #57

Our company has undergone a much-needed reorganization. My friend got laid off, while I got promoted. I'm sad for him but pleased for myself. Now he's pressing me to quit. Is he right?

THE LESSON OF THE AUSTRALIAN CRAB

In Australia there is a certain type of crab used for fish bait. Once caught, they are kept in open buckets on the pier.

These crabs are excellent climbers. Any one of these crabs could easily crawl up the side of the bucket and over the edge to freedom. But the fishermen don't need to worry about this.

Why?

That the crabs don't escape is not for lack of trying. One crab or another is always on his way up, scrambling toward the light.

However, as soon as the crab separates himself from the pile and makes a run for it, the other crabs reach out for him and pull him back down. No crab has ever been known to escape.

Yet.

TOUGH BUSINESS PROBLEM #58

Nothing I'm trying is working right now, even though I'm not doing anything differently from what's worked for me in the past. Why am I being punished?

"A withered poplar that flowers exhausts its energies thereby and only hastens its end."

The *I Ching* teaches us to release that which has already served its purpose so that the cycles of life may proceed and the groundwork for renewal is laid.

In truth, is that which no longer works for you failure—or completion?

INVOCATION FOR ONE IN TRANSITION

May I realize that what feels to be failure is, in truth, an indication that I have already mastered my past levels of success.

My past has given me so much—it is the very vehicle that has carried me to this moment of transition.

I now find myself in a time of growth where I am too much for the systems that once contained me.

I've mistaken punishment for growth as the reality of who I am becoming screams out for my attention:

"Look carefully! It is only your old, outmoded constructions that are dying. Of course it is painful to watch them go—but the truth is that you no longer need them. They are decaying at your feet: How could you not feel grief for the loss of a level of mastery that was once so important to you? But tell the whole truth as you grieve, for you know that something is birthing, too."

Recognizing now that I am in transition, may I let myself feel the grief, loosening my grip on that which is passing.

I place my attention and energy on that which struggles to be born.

TOUGH BUSINESS PROBLEM #59

I've yet to find a meaningful job that fulfills me. Where is it?

If your life was filled with love, opportunities for self-expression and creativity, a wonderful social life, and occasions to give to your community, would it matter whether your job itself was meaningful or fulfilling? Wouldn't it be gift enough to have a livelihood that supports such a rich life?

The issue is not what your job is or isn't doing for you, it's why you are using your job as an excuse to resist getting on with your life. To have sufficient income to support spending your time outside of work with children, family, and friends; to create for the sheer ecstasy of self-expression; to take joy in the growth of your character through challenge and adversity... this is what you want. What's stopping you?

You have a roof over your head. Food on your plate. If you so choose, you can be among the privileged few on this planet who can move beyond issues of survival and begin to explore expanded dimensions of the potential to be more fully alive.

Your job is beneath you? How could that be if every envelope you stuff reminds you of the goodness of life, if every sink you scrub is filled with gratitude for the gift of being alive? When you give up resentment and arrogance, even simple tasks can bring great fulfillment.

An old Japanese saying teaches, "Before enlightenment you sweep the floor. After enlightenment you sweep the floor."

Work, no matter how mundane, can provide opportunities to develop your character. You can practice teamwork, compassion, discipline, humility—some even more easily if the job is "beneath" you.

Ironically the moment you stop requiring that your career deliver fulfillment to you, you empty yourself of your childish demands. And at that moment opportunities beyond your expectations will rush in to fill the void.

If you are working such long hours that you don't have time to pursue a meaningful life, see Tough Business Problem #80.

If you feel you should be farther along in your career than you are right now, see Tough Business Problem #13.

TOUGH BUSINESS PROBLEM #60

I've had it with abusive bosses, clients, suppliers, family, friends, and subordinates. Now what?

All this time you have quietly been growing stronger and stronger. You have patiently waited for the moment to arrive for you to come forward and declare yourself, to demand your rightful respect and dignity.

There are those who would undermine the reclamation of your life and spirit. Perhaps among them are voices whispering within your own mind: *What makes you think you deserve to prevail? You, with all your imperfections and failings?*

Until now you thought that this moment of reclamation could come only when you perfected yourself: you have worked so hard for self-mastery, trying to be good enough to silence those voices that would exploit and undermine you.

But consider this: Your willingness to face things with the self you are today is in truth the very source of your courage and your strength.

"It is only when we have the courage to face things exactly as they are, without any sort of self-deception or illusion, that a light will develop out of events, by which the path to success may be recognized," says the *I Ching*.

Honor your urge for perfection and mastery, but take heed of the *I Ching*'s warning that one can miss the mark not only by trying too little but by trying too hard as well.

"If one overshoots the goal, one cannot hit it. If a bird will not come to its nest but flies higher and higher, it eventually falls into the hunter's net."

You are already good enough. Your willingness to recognize your weaknesses and yet to aspire to a fuller expression of your potential for goodness are attributes of the superior man.

Here is a resolution for you, the good-enough human being, who is ready to hit the mark:

THE GOOD ENOUGH HUMAN BEING'S BILL OF RIGHTS

1. Even if I fear that I am greedy, stupid, foolish, emotional, lazy, and bad, I deserve to have bosses, clients, suppliers, family, friends, and subordinates who respect me.
2. I have the right to protect myself from exploitation.
3. I can take a stand for myself and my beliefs and let the world march to the beat of my drum for a change.
4. I matter.
5. The universe loves and supports me—exactly as I am.
6. The universe has plans for me better than anything I've yet imagined for myself.
7. I trust in the universe and in myself and am grateful for all that has been given to me—as painful as it has been—because it has brought me to this moment.
8. I am a force to be reckoned with.
9. If you don't support my bill of rights with all your heart and all your soul and all your might, then clear out of my way.
10. I trust in the magic and miracle of my life, and no matter how sad and scary it is to leave the familiarity of being abused behind, I look forward with joyful anticipation to what's next.

TOUGH BUSINESS PROBLEM #61

I tried my best, but I let my team down. They understand, but I feel so terrible that I can't face them again. How can I get back on track?

When you have depleted your inner resources, you have one strength yet remaining: the strength to be simple.

Feeling sad about letting down your teammates is a simple emotion. Feeling bad about feeling sad is unnecessarily complicated.

Accepting your team's understanding at face value is simple. Expecting retribution beyond what has already been administered to you is unnecessarily complicated.

Feeling the fear of facing them again is simple. Acting on that fear by seeking ways to avoid them is unnecessarily complicated.

The truth is that people are drawn to those who humbly submit to whatever fate has handed to them. Fate loves emptiness and simplicity and rushes into the void to fill it with light and love.

So the *I Ching* teaches us to understand the time and not to try to cover up our depleted state with empty pretense. "If a time of scanty resources brings out an inner truth, one must not feel ashamed of simplicity. For simplicity is then the very thing needed to provide inner strength for further undertakings."

If in doubt, do a little too much in the direction of the simple, and you will hit the mark.

If your feeling of guilt is justified, see Tough Business Problem #76.

If you feel you've got to get happy before you can get back on track, see Tough Business Problem #88.

TOUGH BUSINESS PROBLEM #62

When I started out, I loved what I was doing. Lately I've burned out and as a result, I'm struggling. Can this endeavor still succeed?

Endeavors are like fire. For them to keep going, they need revitalized vision the way flames need fresh fuel. Untended, the fire will consume all in its path and die away.

To answer your question, you must ask yourself whether there is the tiniest spark of passion that yet remains in you for this. Your gift is that you can still remember what it feels like to have genuine enthusiasm—the memory of times in your life when you knew you could not fail because your energy was the clean, creative stuff of life. If there is a spark of this in you yet remaining, you can still succeed if you tend it properly.

Tending the flame does not necessarily mean rolling up your sleeves and pushing yourself to dig in once again. It may well mean giving yourself a vacation or sabbatical, building in time to revitalize yourself on a regular basis so that you won't burn out again.

Reconnect to your passion and your endeavor will catch fire again.

If you keep trying to do what's worked in the past, but this time it's not working, see Tough Business Problem #58.

If you feel like you can't possibly break away from the office to take the time to revitalize, see Tough Business Problem #79.

7

Integrity

It is not given to every mortal
to bring about a time of outstanding greatness and abundance.
Only a born ruler of men is able to do it, because his will is
directed to what is great.

—The *I Ching*

TOUGH BUSINESS PROBLEM #63

It doesn't seem right that people with flawed integrity should be getting farther ahead than people who are trying to make something of themselves righteously. Why are they succeeding?

You think you see people with flawed integrity succeeding. What you are actually witnessing is individuals with flawed integrity laying the groundwork for their moment of reckoning.

It may take some time, but it is inevitable. People who detour around what they know to be right and good in order to take a shortcut to success can often seem to have seized the competitive advantage. Slick strategies and clever manipulations can dazzle the marketplace, attracting new business, sales, and opportunities. Business communities and relationships flourish around them—some not yet seeing through their own greed or naïvité in order to jump on board, others joining in like sharks at the spoil.

But close ties among individuals who have put their personal needs ahead of the common good only holds up to a certain point. "Close ties may exist also among thieves; it is true that such a bond acts as a force but, since it is not invincible, it does not bring good fortune," teaches the *I Ching*.

"Where the community of interest ceases, the holding together ceases also, and the closest friendship often changes into hate. Only when a bond is based on what is right, on steadfastness, will it remain so firm that it triumphs over everything."

The *I Ching* teaches us about these people by telling us about the apparent success of the swamp plant, which grows fabulously tall overnight, attracting the eye of all who pass.

Nearby, deep within the soil, a tiny acorn sends up a tender shoot. Which plant, over time, contains the greater potential for success?

Come back tomorrow morning and you will discover something

very interesting. The swamp plant is dead—withered and fallen, its flowers already turning to mud. And the acorn? It is continuing to do its quiet, inner work, persevering day in and day out to fulfill its special destiny. Someday it will be a mighty oak—its development will influence the landscape of the entire region.

You know this to be true on some level of being, and yet you are right to stop and consider the question you pose here—one that has occupied philosophers, saints, and mystics through the ages. Your concern indicates that you are struggling nobly with the forces of darkness. But consider this. The *I Ching* teaches that "the best way to fight evil is to make energetic progress in the good."

By using your discomfort over the issue of unfairness as a vehicle of transformation, you are developing spiritual and emotional muscles. You have the opportunity to develop the strength of character necessary to support a true experience of success.

And what is this experience of success I'm talking about? It is an experience of fulfillment—of having and being enough—that is unrelated to any of the external indicators or occurrences that you have used in the past to define whether or not you consider yourself a success.

You can have this experience of success in your life right now. You can assume the feelings you would have if you had already achieved the outcome you'd most like on your issues. And by doing so, you will bring your best possible self to whatever the challenges you face—including having to struggle with the question you raised here today.

There is tremendous power inherent in he who pays heed to the quality and character of the goodness in his inner being. The superior man is like a crane hidden in the shadows of a high hill. While others may sing a more dazzling note, the crane need not even show himself to sound his call; when the crane's young hear its voice, they recognize it and respond.

"This is the echo awakened in men through spiritual attraction," the *I Ching* teaches.

"Whenever a feeling is voiced with truth and frankness, whenever a deed is the clear expression of sentiment, a mysterious and far-reaching influence is exerted. At first it acts on those who are inwardly receptive. But the circle grows larger and larger. The root of all influence lies in one's inner being: given true and vigorous expression in word and deed, its effect is great. The effect is but the reflection of something that emanates from one's own heart."

One's circle expands—and because you share with others the common concerns of humanity, the influence sustains. But this is not something that happens quickly. Instead this requires perseverance over time. Moreover this deeply rooted influence is not something that can be deliberately intended. Your greatest influence, power, and success come only as a side product of who you have become.

The *I Ching* entreats you to use the oak rather than the swamp plant for your inspiration, even if at the moment you've got your head stuck in the dirt while those around you are waving their tendrils giddily about in the air. It takes tremendous faith to stay with your own experience—to trust that your success will come—and that when it does, it will be a success that will stand the test of time.

If you believe this, but the swamp plant in your life seems to be getting more than its fair share of time in the sun, see Tough Business Problem #89.

If you feel guilty because you secretly feel you may deserve to be left in the dark because you've got some swamp plant in you, see Tough Business Problem #60.

TOUGH BUSINESS PROBLEM #64

In a one-time emergency I pinched ten dollars from petty cash for my own personal use. I feel guilty about it, but I'm too embarrassed to confess, and I'm afraid I'll get caught putting it back. What should I do?

The *I Ching* teaches us that only a strong man can stand up to his fate. Even though the amount in question is only ten dollars, you'll have to come clean by telling the truth.

You have already successfully negotiated the first level of honesty that will lead you to the path to success: You have admitted to yourself that you have a problem. And it isn't just about getting caught, is it? You have recognized that you are having a Moral Dilemma. Many people get derailed at this first juncture. They justify taking the money by any way or means possible: "I did work late last week" or "I never did turn in the receipts for my bridge tolls three years ago" or "I should be making more money anyway."

Be grateful for your guilt. This uncomfortable mental state is giving you the gift of realizing that however brilliant and justified your rationalizations, even you aren't buying them. Not only do you admit that you are troubled by what you did, but you confess that it was wrong. Congratulations! You have passed Level One.

Level Two: It is time to tell the truth about yourself. Did I just feel your stomach turn? What a bad, bad horrible person you are! A monster! In fact the world's worst monster! And you know what? That is your self-indulgent, theatrical, grandiose EGO talking. For the real truth is you are HUMAN—no more, no less. And you made a mistake. It won't go away without your taking some action. You know that. And so you are going to have to do something to fix that mistake. That's the truth. Disappointing, isn't it? And so, in this somewhat deflated state, you are to be congratulated once again. You have now passed Level Two and are ready for Level Three.

Level Three: It is time to act—but first you are going to have to deal with your fear. You are ready for the Tough Business Problem all-purpose fear buster that I have named the "then what."

"Then what" works *with* rather than *against* your fears to help you gain the clarity you need to negotiate the tricky terrain of your inner turmoil successfully.

Here's how it works. Quite simply, you let your fears run wild. State the action you plan to take—"I confess," for example. Next ask yourself, "Then what?"

"My boss tells me he's always suspected me of being that kind of person and fires me on the spot."

Then what?

"Word goes out that I am a dishonest person and no other company in the universe will hire me."

Then what?

"I use up my life savings and end up on the streets, homeless."

Then what?

"I end up in a homeless shelter. The head of the homeless shelter notices that I carry the same Filofax that she does, and before long she finds out that I have an MBA from Stanford."

Then what?

"I tell her my sad story—that I am on the streets because I pinched ten dollars from petty cash in order to pay for my cab home after I stayed at work until midnight putting the finishing touches on the company newsletter."

Then what?

"She says I'm her dream come true. The Homeless Society needs someone who can do a newsletter for the shelter. In fact they've just received a grant, and would I be willing to take on the project."

Then what?

"A story about me is picked up by our local newspaper for its human-interest value, and the newsletter ends up winning a Pulitzer Prize."

Then what?

You get the general idea.

Having purged your fears, your willingness to face things exactly as they are must be followed by resolute and persevering action.

Do you really think your boss would fire you if you addressed the matter head-on?

If you are too nervous to do it in person, could you mail your boss ten dollars with a note explaining the situation, devoid of theatrics and with just the right touch of apology?

It takes courage to rectify a mistake—and courage is one quality that most bosses admire and respect.

If you do have the kind of boss who really might fire you for making and then attempting to rectify an all-too-human mistake, see Tough Business Problem #60.

TOUGH BUSINESS PROBLEM #65

I don't think the product I'm selling is the best choice for my customers but I need the commission. What should I do?

You cannot lie to yourself about your values. If you know that what you are doing is wrong—and choose to persist—you will pay a price for it. Let's say that you've understated the situation. Not only is the product you're selling not the best choice for your customer, it's really not going to work for them at all. Meanwhile it's not that you really "need" the commission, it's that you'd like it to pay for that new stereo you've had your eye on. If you persist, you will pay the price of feeling bad. Is this a price you're willing to pay for your stereo?

Of course this is not a perfect world—and choices are rarely so clear-cut. To add to the confusion, consider: Even spiritual literature contends that some prices are worth paying.

Let's take an extreme example to make the point. What if you really are in a survival situation—you have used up all of your savings and your child is ill and needs medical care? Meanwhile the product you represent, although perhaps not the very best choice for your customer, is good enough. Of course you would and should make the sale.

That will not take away from the fact that you will feel badly about what you have done. However, your feelings—happy or bad—are not always a fair indication of whether or not what you are doing is right. Emotions are unreliable indicators. You must, in situations such as the one you describe, call upon some higher authority—your inner wisdom to help you know what to do.

There is a tendency among those of us who choose to follow a spiritual path to take moral shortcuts by simplifying our decision-making process by turning our own authority over to this book, that guru. I don't trust any system that tells me flat out what is right and what is wrong. I believe that it is up to the individual to decide for himself or herself—and not only once but an infinite number of times, in fact each and every moment of his or her life. The *I Ching* teaches us that maintaining a quiet heart is a function of continuous effort— a willingness to do the hard work of staying current with oneself.

This "good life" is not about moral perfection, a brilliant diamond shining deep in our souls. Rather, to fully live a good life is a messy affair, more a throbbing, pulsing mass than a brilliant diamond. We each have a contradictory core teeming with dynamic tension and that alone has the potential to give our lives creativity and meaning. Ironically only by surrendering to the messiness of the process can we hope to find peace.

If you are alive, you will have to pay a price. Make sure you spend what you've got on something really worth having.

If you go ahead and sell the product because you want the stereo and end up feeling guilty about it, see Tough Business Problem #76.

TOUGH BUSINESS PROBLEM #66

If I only had clients in whom I believed one hundred percent, I'd have no clients. How do I come to terms with the conflict between integrity and paying the bills?

When your inner sense of what is right differs from the demands of the time, inner conflict develops. This is not a terrible thing; inner conflict is the dynamic tension of opposites from which all creativity arises. However, when you realize that you are faced with such a discrepancy, you will need great patience, both with yourself and with others. This is not a time to set about accomplishing great things, but a time for subtle influence and improvement.

If you should push for resolution—either by demanding that your clients come up to meet your standards or by turning your back on what you have created in order to look for individuals more in keeping with your beliefs—you may inadvertently cause damage to yourself. Take a lesson from the bird who sought to soar to the sun—only to singe his wings and crash to the earth. You may aspire to greatness for yourself and your clients, but to undertake the noble task of influencing others, your ascent must begin at the place where your duty lies. You must descend to where your nest is and begin from there.

You will need patience and compassion as you discover that the lesson of morality and integrity is not one of perfection but rather one of progress. It is your job, as the individual with a more highly developed sense of what is right, to exert a subtle and persistent influence on those whom fate has put in your charge.

You do not sink to their level, sacrificing your own sense of what is right to pander to them. Neither do you preach or bully. Rather you remain in place as a subtle force—operating with the positive pull of a magnet and allowing them to find inspiration from your example.

Take this approach for some time; see if there is improvement in the situation. Perhaps your clients have been looking for leadership and will find it in the authentic expression of your heart in the workplace. It is also possible that, recognizing that you cannot be moved, they may choose to leave for other situations that they can more easily shape to serve their ends. If so, this will not be a failure—but rather the sacrifice of what no longer serves you. And you will be freed for a higher purpose.

Trust that over time either your clients will rise to join you or others more in keeping with your values and integrity will come to take their place.

If you raise the stakes, and your business falls apart, see Tough Business Problem #19.

If you think it's unfair that people with flawed integrity can make money running a business, see Tough Business Problem #63.

TOUGH BUSINESS PROBLEMS #67

Small amounts of money keep disappearing from the petty-cash box—a quarter here, fifty cents there. It's really bothering me because it means somebody in my department is dishonest. What should I do?

The *I Ching* teaches that the superior man possesses enough greatness of soul to bear with imperfect people. He also possesses the key to the cashbox. Use it.

TOUGH BUSINESS PROBLEM #68

I know that our company is putting out a product that does not live up to its advertising claims. Do I blow the whistle?

When it comes to your question, the authority of the *I Ching* is joined by that other great teacher—the Federal Trade Commission. More and more companies have been discovering that misleading statements and unsubstantiated claims have a way of finding their way into public consciousness.

On a grand scale the weight-loss industry is sizzling painfully in the media spotlight for promises that cannot be substantiated; on a micro level, some of the leading catalog and retail companies have been fined up to ten thousand dollars per violation for not checking out manufacturers' claims about products they have advertised.

While a ten-thousand dollar fine is painful, the damage to the company or industry's reputation can be many times that amount. It could take hundreds of thousands of advertising and public relations dollars to salvage the company's image. In some cases it is possible that the loss of credibility will prove fatal.

So it becomes clear that the decision to exaggerate on advertising claims carries with it tremendous risk. The same life-driven motivation that spurs your marketing department to want to do their best to support themselves and their families by fudging in the first place is the same motivation that will cause them to listen and pay heed to your wise counsel.

If your company's urge to fudge does not come from life-driven though misguided overzealousness, but rather from a conscious and willful breach of integrity, see Tough Business Problem #69.

If you decide to handle this situation by keeping your mouth shut and making a substantial contribution to a socially responsible cause to help offset your guilt, see Tough Business Problem #71.

TOUGH BUSINESS PROBLEM #69

I've been asked by my boss to do something that I consider to be unethical. If I refuse, I'm afraid I'll be fired. If I go along with it, how will I sleep nights?

If you thought that expanded awareness and a spiritual perspective were the keys to making your life easier, I'm sorry to break the news to you: The more in touch with your own integrity you are, the more likely you are to encounter difficult occasions. The "downside" to expanded spiritual awareness is that you may often find yourself marching in step to your own drummer—a musician with more attuned sensibilities about what is fair and right than most of the rest of the band.

Short-term you may find your developed ethical capability a terrible nuisance. Long-term, however, if you keep the beat going long and loud enough, the band might change its direction and begin marching in yours. When this occurs, you will be providing leadership of the highest caliber to your community—whether the company for which you work or your greater community at large. In spiritual language we call this finely tuned sensitivity heroic. The hero is that individual who is willing to stray from the status quo to follow his or her own heart.

The path you choose to take on this issue—and every time a similar issue arises for you—is critically important to your well-being and future success. And it is a situation that will require of you the utmost honesty and courage ... But the answer is not necessarily to blow the whistle. Sometimes it takes your greatest courage not to act.

Here are some things you should consider doing before you make your decision:

- Make sure you tell yourself the truth about the situation, rather than push it aside because it's uncomfortable. Regardless of whether you are going to take immediate action about the issue at hand, watch out for any tendency to rationalize or excuse behavior inconsistent with your own internal standards. If you do this often enough or on a big enough issue, your moral edge may grate through to your very core, damaging your vitality and sense of purpose.

- Doing something that clearly violates your integrity, perhaps causing others harm, will not be worth it to you in either the short run or the long run. By taking a stand you might offer the one bit of common sense that is missing from the situation, tipping the moral balance of your boss, your company, and your community back in the direction of sanity.

- At the same time know that depending on your motivation it can be a legitimate response to sacrifice your impulse to act now in order to be in a more powerful corrective position later, either in this company or elsewhere. It can take great courage to be willing to wait for your moment—possibly for years, getting no external validation or strokes as you do the quiet, vital work of building your own personal groundswell of character and spirit.

  The *I Ching* teaches that it is not a weakness to hold back from a battle with an opponent of superior strength. It is honorable, under the circumstance, to protect one's energy in order to nurture and grow it: "If tempted out of a false sense of honor into an unequal conflict, he would be drawing down disaster upon himself. In a struggle with an enemy of unequal strength, retreat is no disgrace."

- If you know this will be an unequal battle but you are still called to take action, consider creative ways to even the odds. Perhaps you will be inspired to leave the company to join with others to become an activist in the field; perhaps you will want to go back to school to get more knowledge and credibility so that when you do speak out, you will be listened to.

Whether you decide to go along for the time being or to take a stand, either within your company or on the outside, remember always to tell the truth to yourself about what you believe is right. To knowingly choose discomfort—and to have the patience to wait until you feel that the moment is right to act—can also be an act of heroism.

If you decide to become an activist and miss the big salary, see Tough Business Problem #15.

If your heart is calling you to become the whistle blower, but your family is pressuring you not to stick your neck out, see Tough Business Problem #42.

TOUGH BUSINESS PROBLEM #70

Now that they've trained me, I see how I could do better by running a competitive company—keeping all the profits for myself. Don't I have the right to watch out for my own interests in this?

Spirituality is not about being nice—it is about being fully alive. In fact only when you approach your career with what the *I Ching* calls the "greed of a hungry tiger, spying about with sharp eyes," do you have the degree of zeal it takes to succeed.

But there's a catch: The "insatiable craving" of the tiger is worthy of respect only when "the tiger is not working for himself but for the good of all."

The desire to play a bigger game is stirring in your heart. Set yourself in competition with a mentor and you set forces greater than yourself in motion. There are those who may condemn you. There are those who may admire you. Only you can know your innermost motivation.

If you hope to avert guilt, before you make your move, confront these following five questions honestly and courageously. Only when you are certain that your answer is yes in every case will your venture provide you the experience of success you are looking for.

- Do you plan to found your company with assets and resources that have been honestly acquired through your own merit, or are you exploiting the work of others?
- Through the relationship you model with your boss, are you creating a standard that you would want your own future employees to emulate in all of their dealings with you into the distant future?
- Are you grateful for all that you've received, seeing yourself as

building upon rather than damaging the legacy of those who came before you?

- Are you doing this for the good of all—or are you working for yourself alone?
- Does your heart tell you that you have no choice but to proceed?

If your answer to all five of these questions is yes, then your desire to run a competitive firm is life-driven and you should proceed with the zeal of a hungry tiger.

If you would like some advice on how to break this news to your boss, see Tough Business Problem #4.

If your main motivation is the urge to compete, see Tough Business Problem #89.

8

In Search of Greatness

The wise man gladly leaves fame to others. He does not seek to have credited to himself things that stand accomplished, but hopes to release active forces; that is, he completes his works in such a manner that they may bear fruit for the future.

—The *I Ching*

TOUGH BUSINESS QUESTION #71

In order to be socially responsible, what percentage of my work life and salary should go toward good works?

You want to know what percentage you should give? Five percent, ten percent—it won't be enough. Life-driven business demands more of you. It won't settle for a share of your profits or proceeds. It won't be satisfied with matching funds or donations for each item you buy or sell.

How many socially responsible companies give a percentage of their profits to charitable works ostensibly in the name of generosity but really in exchange for big tax write-offs and massive publicity? Touting their spiritual attainment in full-page ads in newspapers and magazines, they brag about making contributions to this or that cause. The public is seduced into feeling good buying their products—even if it contains herbs farmed by indentured slaves in Third World countries or carry trendy labels that artificially inflate the cost of the merchandise. Yet we honor these merchants for their big hearts, feeling guilty if we do not match their five or ten percent with comparable contributions of our own.

Life-driven business wants more. It wants one hundred percent. That's right. Life-driven business demands that you give social responsibility everything you've got.

If you are a professional—a lawyer, for instance—you take on clients who are worthy of your time and attention. The clients may or may not be the poor and disenfranchised. But they should invariably be individuals for whom a favorable verdict equates to your own sense of justice—rather than merely your ability to manipulate the judicial system. Life-driven work is the greatest contribution you can make—of much more value to the greater community than spending your work life exploiting the system, then assuaging your guilt with a su-

240

perfluous tithe of money or time to this or that worthwhile group.

If you are a manufacturer, you make a product you are proud of. You reveal rather than hide the ingredients or materials, the strengths and the weaknesses. You resist the urge to charge what you can get away with, gouging the public to underwrite the tab for getting your name on the library at a local university—but rather you ask only for what is just enough. If you are a movie producer, you choose scripts that avoid pandering to and inciting humanity's lower instincts, trusting that you can make a good product without resorting to exploitation and trusting too that the public will support your work. Whatever your profession may be, you can run your work life with social responsibility by asking what you can contribute with your career or company.

It is contribution enough to make a decent living performing a simple task that causes others no harm, asking only for fair compensation and leaving you free to have time and space for loving others—your children, your spouse, your friends.

When you run your work life on the principles of life-driven business, your heart will be full. Out of the fullness of your heart you will spontaneously want to give to others. It will be a natural and effortless part of your workday and life.

When you truly dedicate your life to the greater good, your total work life becomes a socially responsible contribution. Your salary goes to a worthy cause: the care and support of a socially responsible person. You.

If you think there's an inherent conflict between integrity and paying the bills, see Tough Business Problem #66.

TOUGH BUSINESS PROBLEM #72

I want my employees to like me, so I'll do anything to avoid giving them negative feedback. How can I still be a nice guy but get them to perform to my standards?

Understand that every time you resist giving honest feedback now—when your subordinates have the chance to make a correction—you increase the odds of having to fire them down the road. Which do you think is nicer, to give negative feedback now or to fire them later?

If the subordinate in question is your boss's nephew, see Tough Business Problem #30.

TOUGH BUSINESS PROBLEM #73

No matter how hard I try to conduct inspiring staff meetings, they fall flat. What can I do to inspire my staff?

An entire branch of the management-consulting industry has been built on helping businesses identify, nurture, and sustain the characteristics of a good leader who can inspire his or her subordinates. The definition of what these characteristics are has varied from one year to the next. Should the leader have superior technical expertise? Market knowledge? Should he or she be a tough disciplinarian, inspiring the troops to exceed the limitations of their existing expectations? Or is a softer approach the way to go—a more nurturing, compassionate relationship to subordinates?

In tackling the response to your question, I am inspired by Rolf Osterberg, who recently considered the issue of leadership in his book *Corporate Renaissance*. In brief he declined to play the game, believing that it would be wrong to attempt to define the characteristics of leadership in this way. "Why? Because we are discussing human beings, not human beings in a certain situation. So, what we are really searching for is a definition of a good human being. From that I abstain."

What we do know of Osterberg's leader is that he or she manages in a new paradigm, where "the measure of a man's work is not what he has obtained from it, but what he has become of it.

"We do not exist to survive, but to live. We do not exist to obtain things—to amass money, to gain position and power, to collect possessions and thereby prove our worth to ourselves and others; we exist to learn, to develop and to grow as human beings."

In this new paradigm the leader does not take classes in order to become inspirational—rather he or she has earned a leadership role because he or she is inspired.

Here is an invocation for leadership of a new kind:

INVOCATION FOR INSPIRING OTHERS

May I recognize that when I inspire people—it is not because of what I do, but because of who I am.

I inspire people when I share my genuine enthusiasm for life by listening and receiving as well as by giving and telling.

When I have the courage to say what needs to be said, remembering that it is my actions not my words that carry the message.

When I am willing to expose more of who I really am with trust and vulnerability, even when it stretches me beyond my own comfort level.

When I remember that inspiring people has nothing to do with what I want *from* them, but rather has to do with opening the space *for* them to move beyond their own fears to go for what they really want.

TOUGH BUSINESS PROBLEM #74

Would my company benefit from a more democratic approach to management?

The new-paradigm business ethic rightfully decries the autocratic, patriarchal hierarchy as the dinosaur of business-management systems. "Equality and respect" are the new watchwords, as companies turn their organizational charts into social experiments.

But equality and respect are not easy concepts to grasp—and are even more challenging to implement. Here a superficial understanding will prove disastrous. Such was the case with one company, a candy-store chain, reeling giddily from quick and early success; its executives decided to open up the management decision-making process to the entire company. They had seen this as a way to decentralize the decision-making process, empowering each individual within the company to respond more quickly to the ever-increasing demands faced by the rapidly growing chain.

Each member of the workforce was given an equal vote—from the newest employee to the guy who had had the original vision, even mortgaging his house to fund the operation.

For a day or two, individuals at all levels of the operation basked in the freedom. What they were doing, they told the reporters who came to cover the story for the business pages of the local newspapers, was the way it could and should be for all companies.

But truth be told, in short order they were deeply mired in trying to deal with dozens of issues—some valid, some the result of personal whims—unable and unwilling to discriminate between them. Meetings were held about meetings, and rival camps began forming. The company's forward movement came to an abrupt halt. Top management retrenched and took back the reins. Order was restored—but at great cost. Many of the employees left. Turnover remained a major problem for years afterward.

Many a well-intentioned company has quickly descended from order to chaos—all in the name of equality.

Consider instead an alternate definition of equality. Equality means simply that everyone in the organization has the equal opportunity to develop their skills and abilities, thus earning the right to take on more leadership responsibilities.

The *I Ching* teaches that "among mankind there are necessarily differences in elevation; it is impossible to bring about universal equality. But it is important that differences in social rank should not be arbitrary and unjust, for if this occurs, envy and class struggle are the inevitable consequences."

Differences in rank generate respect rather than strife when they are based on qualities that reflect inner worth as well as external performance. These can be both intuitively and objectively judged, taking into consideration such criteria as loyalty and commitment to the organization, passion and purpose, comfort with risk taking, and the courage and humility that are hallmarks of the true leader. Not everyone has developed these qualities in himself or herself to the same degree.

If the urge to democratize your company was born out of discomfort with the way things are, perhaps the place to begin the process of establishing a more just organization is for top management to take an honest look at themselves. Is their power and authority reflective of their inner worth? Confucius says that "weak character combined with an honored place will seldom escape disaster."

If this is the case with your company's leadership, are they willing to rectify the situation by doing the internal work they need to undertake in order to rise to the occasion? If not, are they willing to redistribute responsibility and authority with those who are willing?

Once that is the case, your organization will be healthy and vital— whatever shape your organizational chart eventually takes.

If you are the one holding power illegitimately in your company, see Tough Business Problem #76.

TOUGH BUSINESS PROBLEM #75

Help me do the right thing. I decided to work part-time, but I've been here longer and I have more responsibility. My colleague works full-time, so the answer to this question will have more impact on her quality of life than on mine. The question: Who gets the better office?

The *I Ching* takes the issue of land disbursement (including that which takes the particular form of an office in a high-rise) seriously. As noble as your expressed desire to be fair in this situation is, you seem to have missed the point entirely.

Assuming that your associate can find office space elsewhere in the building, who gets which office does not have anything to do with quality of life. Rather it has to do with who has been sanctioned to wield authority.

You are trying to administer justice in this situation. Before you can administer justice, however, you need objectivity. You need a commitment to the truth. The tone of your question implies that you feel that your contribution to the workplace has been diminished by the fact that you work part-time. Listen closely: The value you provide to your company and the power you wield on its behalf have nothing to do with how many hours you work.

Your power is a reflection of the qualities you have come to represent to your company. Your presence in the company over time demonstrates that you have loyalty, commitment, and perseverance. Your decision to work part-time means, additionally, that you have the wisdom to balance work with other aspects of your life in order to bring the most vital person possible to your office each day, that you have the courage to ask for what you want and to hold your own regardless of what others might think, that you have earned the right to benefit from whatever flexibility your company has to offer. They think it's worthwhile to bend to your needs in order to retain your knowledge, your expertise, and the very characteristics that have provoked your move to part-time employment.

Your associate quite simply has not earned the right to wield the power you have. Give someone the gift of office perks and privileges they have not rightfully earned, and you can rest assured about one thing: Power will be abused.

You want to administer justice? Then tell the truth about who you are. In the long run false humility makes as many problems for everybody as ego. In fact false humility may be the most virulent form of arrogance—the self-important and grandiose expression of modesty that has the audacity to deny who and what you are and to betray you, your associate, and your company by giving away your power under false pretenses.

It is better to leave a power spot empty than to give it to someone who has overreached their own status. Let it serve as an informal lunchroom, an extra conference space, even storage. But don't give your power—or your office space—away.

If you tell her you're going to keep your office and you think you see resentment flash across her face, see Tough Business Problem #23.

If you think keeping the best office isn't democratic, see Tough Business Problem #74.

If your boss thinks your colleague should get the better office, see Tough Business Problem #60.

TOUGH BUSINESS PROBLEM #76

I did something that I am right to feel guilty about. I've done what I can to make amends, but the bad feelings won't go away.

INVOCATION FOR THE RESTORATION OF INTEGRITY

Shaken by the confrontation of aspects of myself that I do not like, I surrender to the admission that imperfection is the human condition.

Now that I've done what I can to rectify my errors, I humbly ask for compassion and faith to be restored.

Not as a child, saying "Here is my authentic self. You have to love me."

Rather, by saying "Here is my authentic self, flaws and all. While I prefer you love me, I am willing to take the consequences."

My guilt shows the way, fueling my heart with resolve, helping me expand to my greater self, a compassionate and loving being bigger than my anger, fear, and regret.

Big enough to encompass it all.

In this moment of reconcilliation, I affirm that I will not be shaken from my right to be whole again—including my right to make mistakes, my right to make amends for my mistakes, and my right to reclaim my integrity.

If you are still thrashing about in the underbelly of your emotions even though everybody else has already forgiven you, see Tough Business Problem #61.

If your guilt is keeping you awake nights, see Tough Business Problem #91.

TOUGH BUSINESS PROBLEM #77

A client says he's withholding payment because my results disappointed him. As a professional I get paid for providing services—I don't guarantee results. How do I fight him?

The best way to resolve a problem is to head it off before it has time to lay down roots. You can do this by spending more time in the beginning educating your client about the fact that you get paid for work undertaken, not results. If you are reluctant to address the issue of guarantees with your client, ask yourself if you sense that your client will have trouble with this concept and possibly not sign on. If so, it is even more important to address this up front. It's better to clarify the terms of your relationship and risk his not signing on as a client than to do your clarification in a court of law after you've failed to collect on work already done.

That said, you've got to deal with the situation at hand. How you fight him depends on whether you truly feel that you are in the right—not only in terms of whether or not you did good-enough work but whether or not you were courageous and wise enough up front to educate him.

If you aren't convinced you did everything you could, you will be tempted to spread ill will about him in the form of gossip, rumors, and complaints; you will do what you can to slyly undermine him—but you won't take your conflict out into the open. In time your negative approach will backfire and you will be injured.

If you fell short on either education or work performed, the more heroic route is to sit down with your client and tell the whole truth: what you did accomplish and where you faltered. Under these circumstances most clients will be willing to negotiate. You can offer either to work extra hours to close the gap between expectation and delivery or to rectify the bill.

Even if you feel yourself to be clearly in the right, the *I Ching* instructs that you should still be willing to meet your client part way: "To carry on the conflict to the bitter end has evil effects even when one is in the right, because the enmity is then perpetuated." The goal should be to resolve the issue as quickly and cleanly as possible, even if that means you do not collect the entire amount. You cut your losses to free your energy to create new opportunities, rather than getting mired in old failures. Negotiate an amount that takes into consideration the value moving on will have to you.

That doesn't mean you don't ever go to court. You do, but only if you cannot negotiate to a conclusion with your client that satisfies you on even this modest level. There is after all a matter of principle involved. If you did educate your client adequately in the beginning and if you did the work to the best of your ability and with the best of intentions, then you need to draw a line in the sand. If the amount to be collected justifies it, hire a lawyer to pursue the money owed you—even if his or her fee will offset most of the gain. Some lawyers will work for a percentage of money collected. If the money is too small an amount to interest a lawyer in an arrangement of this type, take the case up in small-claims court—even if you have to reduce the amount to be collected in order to qualify.

If you don't feel you are clearly in the right but are usually too hard on yourself, see Tough Business Problem #90.

If you don't feel you are clearly in the right and are just hoping to get away with something like everybody else does, see Tough Business Problem #63.

TOUGH BUSINESS PROBLEM #78

A valuable employee made a stupid mistake that will cost the company thousands of dollars. Who pays?

You value your employee—even though he made a stupid mistake. This shows two fundamentals of great leadership: compassion and clarity—Now you look to administer justice in this situation, rightly understanding that to do nothing would be too weak, yet to ask the employee to pay the entire amount would be too harsh.

The key to administering justice in this situation is to ask yourself what it is you hope to achieve. If your company is not in a survival mode, the money involved should not be the issue. Every business must operate on the principle that mistakes will be made, stupid and otherwise. Just as you must build up capital to cover natural disasters, such as fires and earthquakes, so should you be ready to cover man-made ones as well. However, although you mentally prepare yourself to cover your employee's mistake, you must not relinquish your right to use this occasion to deliver the message to *all* of your employees that carelessness, no matter who the deliverer may be, bears consequences.

Believe it or not, you can do so in such a way that the bond of loyalty and respect between you and your employees is strengthened by the interaction.

Here's how: If your employee is as valuable as you believe him to be, you can trust that he is as dismayed and upset about the mistake as you are. Take the leap of faith that he, too, would like it to be rectified fairly, as much for his peace of mind as for your own. You have this in common. So why not reach out to him and make him a partner in the decision-making process? What should the consequences be? Let him think about it and offer his opinion concerning assessment of damages.

253

By including him you reaffirm the bond of trust that put him in a position of responsibility that made a mistake of this magnitude possible in the first place. Knowing that he still has your respect, he has the potential to emerge from this ordeal with his spirit undamaged. He has been given the opportunity to retain the confidence he needs from you in order to continue taking risks and functioning fully at the cutting edge of his growth on behalf of you and your company.

With this degree of acceptance don't be surprised if the employee exceeds your hopes and expectations and offers to pay for it all. I have seen even the most hardened boss melt under such circumstances. Often, so grateful is he to have an employee who takes his responsibility seriously that the amount proposed by the employee is lightened substantially or even forgiven fully.

You and your employee have been given a great gift, one worth many times the potential cost to either of you: the opportunity to demonstrate faith in each other. The relationship you have the potential to forge together will be one that has shown itself to stand the test of hard times. With such an employee you will have a foundation of mutual trust upon which truly great enterprises can be built.

If you are the employee in question and you think only a fool would offer to pay for his mistake and that the new paradigm is a bunch of hogwash, see Tough Business Problem #94.

If you are the employee and you can't shake the guilt, even though you've offered to pay your share, see Tough Business Problem #61.

9

Balance and Productivity

The superior man reduces that
which is too much, and augments that which is too little. He
weighs things and makes them equal.

—The *I Ching*

TOUGH BUSINESS PROBLEM #79

**I've got too many conflicting demands in each workday.
How can I set priorities without dropping any balls?**

You do not need to add the extra task of setting priorities to your
already burdensome schedule, which would require that you take valuable time to divide your workload into A, B, and C's—and then do
it all anyway. True prioritization is about making difficult choices,
taking gutsy stands.

Before you can make your best decisions, you will have to remember who you are when you are at your best. Are you at your best
when you are reactive and fearful? Of course not. Therefore I am
going to ask you to do something very gutsy, something that will take
great wisdom, courage, and faith.

Push away from your desk.

Walking slowly and deliberately, leave your office and go outside.

Let some fresh air into your closed system, restoring perspective
and clarity. Take a long, leisurely walk—notice the clouds, the wind
on the back of your neck, the feel of the pavement beneath your feet.

Now that you are beginning to breathe again, you can see how
reactive and exhausted you are. How often have you made foolish
mistakes it took extra time to correct in this state? How often do you
compulsively tear into busywork that could easily be delegated or
dumped? Is it easier to say yes to unfair demands out of exhaustion,
than to stand up for yourself? How long has it been since you've had
a creative insight or an intuitive flash—those simple and elegant shortcuts that used to come to you naturally and effortlessly when you
were inspired, not exhausted? Are you beginning to remember how it
feels when you are primed rather than depleted? How productive you
can be?

As you continue your walk, consider what pace you can set for

256

yourself that honors your physical, emotional, and spiritual aspects. Walk too slowly and you get bored. Walk too fast and you exhaust yourself. What speed—what dynamic degree of tension—is the one that allows you to be at your best? Like your life, this walk, is not a race to be won in the end. It is a process. Take time to appreciate what you see along the way. Is there a flower poking up through the cement? A bird picking at a seed? Walk just fast enough so that you can appreciate each step and are eager to see what new surprises come up along the way. Some will be external like the drop of rain that brushes your nose; some will be internal, like that funny little idea, that great breakthrough realization that will cut your workload by one-third!

Only when your heart has slowed its pace are you ready to begin the work of setting priorities. Start with an honest assessment of your available time. How much time are you being paid to work? How much more time can you afford to contribute—without injuring your need to preserve and protect the time you need outside of work hours to refuel and revitalize?

How often do you need a break? Do you need and take your full lunchtime to revitalize, or do you push your way through it with a power lunch? If you must work through lunch, relating to others as part of your business culture, do you give yourself downtime after lunch to recover?

If you are concerned about the time this takes, remember that when you are at your best, you are more willing to take risks. As a result you will spend less time in meetings about meetings, less time getting sign-offs on memos designed to spread the blame should the project run into trouble. When you are at your best, you find the courage to say no to projects that waste your time. You protect yourself from individuals and demands that take you off course. You have more time to accomplish the work that you have been hired to do.

If, after considering all this, you realize that even if you were at your best, there would still not be enough time in the day to complete your work, you will find the courage to address your boss, knowing that you have the right to ask for an appropriate workload and proper assistance.

How should you set priorities? There is only one item on your list: You must commit yourself to taking your own vitality seriously.

Make this your only priority and you will achieve your greatest success—not despite your decision to honor your physical, emotional, and spiritual needs, but *because* you have decided to honor them.

If you cut yourself some slack in order to bring your best to the workplace, and your boss tells you that if you have time to take a break, you must not be busy enough, see Tough Business Problem #81.

If this is your first job, see Tough Business Problem #8.

TOUGH BUSINESS PROBLEM #80

I've got a full-time job that saps so much of my energy that there's nothing left in me to pursue my life's passion: sculpture. What can I do about this?

Get a part-time job.

If you think it's not fair that in order to pursue your passion, you have to sacrifice your lifestyle, see Tough Business Problem #52.

TOUGH BUSINESS PROBLEM #81

Our company has supplied each of us with a private arsenal of computer notebooks and cellular car phones in order to wage hand-to-hand combat with the competition. At first we were thrilled, but now we realize that we are expected either to be at work or to be available for business communication twenty-four hours a day. Help!

If business is like war, then communication between campaign headquarters and the troops on the front line is of critical importance, right?

But there's a problem with this thesis. Who says business has to be like war? As you are discovering, the thrill of seeing business as a battlefield can be seductive, but it is ultimately damaging. Although some businesses encourage the hiring and development of kamakaze executives, who believe that their jobs bring them face-to-face with issues worth sacrificing their lives for, the truth is that most issues faced by those of us in business on a daily basis are not worth dying for. Additionally the issues are often more complex than simple win-lose, all-or-nothing, us-versus-them thinking.

A healthier approach is to see business as a creative expression of life, rather than a destructive reaction to it. Creativity is an organic, life-driven process, and the creative process not only allows but demands periodic bouts of chaos and uncertainty. You mull over possibilities, try new things, take risks. You give a little, you take a little. You make some points here, lose some there. This sale gets made, this one blown. Over all, over time, your inner process remains nurtured and respected.

Vital, organic people build vital, organic corporations. And what do embattled people build? Companies that are at war.

We have forgotten what business is about. Business is the vehicle through which individuals make a fair contribution of their time and energy to the community in exchange for a fair amount of money on which to live.

If the marketplace is not willing to pay your company what it considers to be a fair price for a fair contribution of time and energy, your management has a choice. It can, as your company has so chosen, blame the "enemy" in the name of "global competition," "the economy," and the "increasingly competitive marketplace" in order to avoid confronting the fact that the company has already failed in its mission. They are choosing to keep the game going by asking you to compensate for their inadequacies by giving far more than your fair share—working around the clock, and asking your staff to do the same—in order to preserve the illusion that your company is still viable.

If you are an adrenaline junkie who has let your civilian life recede before the seductive battle high of business as war, this approach has great appeal. Not only do you get to preserve the illusion that the company you work for is still viable, but you get to live perpetually on the edge of all-absorbing crisis. Whole companies are fueled by such daily infusions of adrenaline. Sacrifice your ordinary life for the illusion-driven work style long enough, and you may soon no longer feel fully alive unless you are in the midst of crisis.

The alternative choice for your company is to reconsider, through a painful but potentially productive process of introspection, whether what your company is offering really has as much value for the community as was originally hoped. Based on what your company finds, it can reevaluate and walk the hero's path, doing whatever it takes to re-create a viable role for itself that will be supported by the marketplace.

Meanwhile here's my advice to you: When you're done with a fair day's work, unplug the electronic notebook and turn off the phone.

Unless of course you want to use your arsenal to help you wage a battle worth fighting for—finding a new job with a life-driven rather than a fear-driven company.

And one final piece of guidance: When you go for that better position, look for a company that hasn't already failed.

If you turn your machines off and get fired before you have the opportunity to resign, see Tough Business Problem #97.

If you are an adrenaline junkie, see Tough Business Problem #84.

If you're not an adrenaline junkie but you like your job too much to risk standing up for your needs, see Tough Business Problem #52.

TOUGH BUSINESS PROBLEM #82

My boss gives me more to do than anyone could possibly accomplish in the number of hours he's paying me for. Now he's set up a meeting to give me even more assignments. How should I handle this?

He says, "Jump"—and you say, "How high?" This is an old, old pattern for you. Recognizing this, there's both good news and bad. The bad news first: You can't stop old emotions. The good news? You *can* stop old patterns of responding to old emotions.

When you feel the urge to jump, do something very tricky in its place: breathe. Break the threat-response circuit. Take a deep breath. Feel your feet against the floor. Feel the weight of gravity connecting you to the center of the earth. When you become centered again— mentally, physically, and spiritually—you can disengage from automatic reactions and take charge. It will be even easier for you if you come prepared.

Your boss is asking you to do more than he's paying you for. Knowing this in advance, you've got a choice. Perhaps it is worth·it to you to give him what he's asked for. Maybe the "extra" assignments are actually the ones that are most interesting to you—the ones that represent the growth in the position. It may well be worth sacrificing your hours to build new skills and improve your résumé. Particularly if it is early in your career, your boss can be enormously helpful to you on the way up. If so, even taking into consideration the fact that he is asking for more than he's paying you for in terms of salary, it could still be a fair trade.

If, on the other hand, there is no value to be gained—other than keeping your position—you are being exploited. But understand, your boss may not even be aware that he is doing this to you. It is up to you to set boundaries for the relationship.

The next time you are given more than your fair share of assignments, approach your boss to ask for a strategic-planning process meeting.

As you prepare for this meeting, assess each assignment and the amount of time it will take to complete. Take into consideration the pace at which you work your best. If you know that time-consuming, last-minute emergencies always tend to crop up, estimate these under the category of "miscellaneous."

Now lay out all the assignments on a page labeled "Strategic Plan."

When you come face-to-face with your boss, take the lead by suggesting that you and he together select those assignments that it is most important to complete in the time allotted. If you work a part-time schedule of twenty hours a week, for instance, stop when you and he have selected what you estimate to be twenty hours worth of assignments from your plan.

If there are additional assignments left over, your boss has a choice: He can either pay you to cover the additional hours it will take to complete the leftover items he still wants done; if you are not willing to work additional hours, he can have someone else in the company do it, or bring in outside help; or he can replace some of the items already selected with other items that he now realizes may be more important for you to accomplish.

In this way you can avoid an adversarial relationship and work in tandem toward the same goal: a fair and productive relationship.

If you feel guilty because you have a life, see Tough Business Problem #85.

If the whole industry in which you work is structured around regular after-hours contributions of time, and you don't want to quit but you still want a more reasonable workload, see Tough Business Problem #81.

TOUGH BUSINESS PROBLEM #83

Some mornings I walk into the office and from the moment I first lay eyes on the receptionist, I dislike everybody and everything I see. They can't all be so bad— especially since just the day before, I liked everybody and everything just fine. Help me make it through the day!

Your brain, beleaguered as you may feel it to be, is making valuable linkages. You recognize, for instance, that it is improbable that overnight all the people you work with here suddenly become lazy bums, ingrates, jerks, or any of the other names you want to call them.

Many people, when swept up in such a highly charged state, think that they have to do something about it. Many a bad mood has had its sacrificial lamb—when in fact the bad mood had nothing to do with external reality. How many staff meetings have been called "to clear the air," how many employees reprimanded or fired, when in fact the air that needed clearing was inside the boss's brain?

It is important to be able to tell when and when not to take external reality seriously. If you become disturbed day after day in the presence of one particular individual, for instance, that is a good indication that there is something you need to be paying attention to in your relationship to that person.

If, on the other hand, you become disturbed by everybody on one particular day, I can assure you of one thing: The problem is not "out there." If my word doesn't suffice, and you want an additional reality check, take a trusted associate aside and ask, "Is something up? Or is it just my mood?"

If your hook comes up empty, take a time-out before you push into the heart of your day to inventory your own inner landscape. Are you upset about something? In the workplace? In your home life? How are you feeling emotionally, physically, spiritually?

If you discover that something is bothering you, deal with it as best you can within the context of the workday. If it is not appropriate to do anything about it then and there—and if you can't take time away from the office to handle it—go ahead with your regular workday, but take extra care not to let your problems spill over onto innocent bystanders.

If you can't put your finger on the problem but are still disturbed, take a leap of faith for the time being and decide that maybe there really *isn't* something you need to handle "out there." This does not mean you are condemned to live your day out among jerks and bums. But to transform your workplace, you will need to transform yourself.

I am going to share with you a powerful spiritual exercise that can turn around the most fetid of foul moods. (This was taught to me by a Zen teacher. I have found this practice to be so effective, I have made it a daily practice—a sort of insurance policy for interpersonal relationships.) You don't need to believe it is going to work. You only need to act "as if" it will work.

What is this transformative exercise? Simply this: Be especially gracious to the next person who crosses your path. It could be your boss. It could be the mailman. Whoever it may be, take an extra moment to give him or her a compliment, inquire about his family or vacation plans, express gratitude for something genuine that you have neglected to mention.

As you turn your focus toward expanding yourself to give to others rather than retracting to judge or retreat from them, you will find your positive energy and rapport returning to you manyfold. There's no need to "get to the bottom" of the problem before you take this on. And you don't have to wait until tomorrow, hoping to find the right side of your bed.

Like health returning after an illness, transformation is always just one spontaneous act of kindness away.

If every day is one of those days, see Tough Business Problem #84.

TOUGH BUSINESS PROBLEM #84

I'm desperate. I'm overwhelmed. My work life is a disaster. What should I do?

Before taking any action, ask yourself this critically vital question:

IS THERE ANY CHANCE
THAT I AM TAKING THINGS
A LITTLE TOO SERIOUSLY RIGHT NOW?

If the answer is no, you're not taking things too seriously right now, see Tough Business Problem #100.

TOUGH BUSINESS PROBLEM #85

I resent how often my boss calls me at home at night with an emergency report due by ten A.M. the next morning. I thought I liked my work, but isn't my lack of commitment telling me something different?

Moments of grand-scale heroism—whether it be pulling an all-nighter to get a report done in time or getting up at dawn every day for a week to complete the successful harvest of a fragile crop—can add a dash of excitement to any life from time to time. The trouble comes when you rise to the occasion and then forget to come back down when it's all over.

If you happen to be a relatively sane individual trying to live a normal life in the midst of a culture that condones or celebrates the state of perpetual crisis as proof of commitment and responsibility, you do indeed have a problem. But, unlike those above, beside, and quite possibly below you who have lost perspective, you have something else. You've got a life.

That is something that is right about you. Something that works. Something it is okay to want and to have. Something that healthy companies want for their employees. Something that other employees in other situations have.

Once you recover from the sense of guilt you have felt by not fully buying into your boss's program, you can begin to see your desire to go home at a decent hour, to have your evenings free for relationship and relaxation, to have weekends for creativity and entertainment, as a different kind of heroism than the grand-scale histrionics that pass for heroics in most companies.

Freed from guilt, able to honor your desires as normal, you can attain clarity about your boss's and quite possibly your company's culture. And out of clarity you will be able to take action.

Let's consider some of the possibilities.

Perhaps your more relaxed approach to work is consistent with your company's culture and it is quite simply your misfortune to have found the one boss in the place who is an adrenaline junkie. If you have a good relationship, you could have a heart-to-heart with your boss. Let him know that although you are willing to respect his work style, you find it injurious to your well-being to work the way he does. Assure him that while you are of course willing to rise to the occasion, you work better and more efficiently when you are able to relax and revitalize after work and on weekends. Since there is undoubtedly a growing body of evidence in your company's disability-claims department that will substantiate your position, you might just grab his ear.

Get to him early enough—before you've become sarcastic or burnt out with resentment—and you might even be able to enroll him in accommodating your request. The success of this approach depends on how much he values you and your work—and how much he trusts you to maintain your high standards. He might not love it that you go home at five-thirty and unplug the phone while he and others on your team keep their candles burning till the wee hours of the night, but he could very well come to respect you.

On the other hand, you may well discover that he does prefer to have people on his staff who share his work style. If you address this potential area of conflict head-on, before either of you starts acting out in reaction to unspoken differences, he may help you find a place elsewhere in the company with a boss whose quality-of-life considerations more closely match your own.

If, on the other hand, it is not just your boss but your whole company that is in perpetual crisis, it's time to ask yourself if whatever it is you are doing for a living is worth the sacrifice. Do you share the company line that opening up a new market for cured salami is worth the sacrifice of your life? Do you believe that your company has made good decisions concerning investment in the number of staff people required to do the necessary work versus the investment in big salaries at the top of the pyramid? Do you really share your company's values?

Believe in your company's organizational and management philosophy—and abilities?

If not, you should not be worrying about being fired—you should be figuring out how and when to give notice. This, too, can be one of those occasions to which you must rise.

If you decide to approach your boss about your feelings and he tells you that your company is in a war and that to quit on him now would be treason, see Tough Business Problem #81.

If you feel your boss might be willing to work with you to put together a better working relationship, see Tough Business Problem #82.

If your boss decides to fire you before you have a chance to find a position in a saner company, see Tough Business Problem #60.

TOUGH BUSINESS PROBLEM #86

Things are going great for me. I managed to bail out of my former firm just before they went under—taking their key accounts with me as the basis for the new company I've launched. But now my spouse is threatening to leave if I don't find more time for family life. How can I get him to lighten up on me?

You say things are "going great" for you. But this is a judgment that cannot be made in isolation. In order to know whether you can expect your good fortune to continue, you need to examine not only your own experience, but the effects of your conduct on others around you—the people you work with, your friends, your family.

The *I Ching* teaches that "if the effects are good, then good fortune is certain. No one knows himself. It is only by the consequences of his actions that a man can judge what he is to expect."

What are your effects? Is there joy and light, inspiration and fellowship where you are? In your previous situation did your impact on others help them thrive? Has your success to date been a testimony to the higher aspirations of humanity—service and support—rather than the lower human capabilities—greed and competitiveness?

In your family life are your relationships whole and healthy? Are your spouse and your children benefiting from their relationship with you? Are your children thriving?

Is your life bearing good fruit—or rotten?

Only when your answers to these questions are affirmative can you know that things really are ''going great'' for you and whether or not you can expect good fortune to follow.

If your answer to all these questions is affirmative, see Tough Business Problem #42.

If you answered no and now your remorse is keeping you awake nights, see Tough Business Problem #91.

TOUGH BUSINESS PROBLEM #87

I've got a report due tomorrow. To finish it on time, I'll have to miss my child's third-grade play. She's only in the chorus. What should I do?

Consider:

WHICH CHOICE WILL HAVE
THE GREATER RAMIFICATIONS
FIVE YEARS FROM NOW?

If you feel that this incident is indicative of the fact that your life is an overwhelming disaster, see Tough Business Problem #84.

10

Inner Peace and Spiritual Practice

The influence on others must
proceed from one's own person. In order to be capable of
producing such an influence, one's words must have power,
and this they can have only if they are based on something
real, just as flame depends on its fuel.

—The *I Ching*

TOUGH BUSINESS PROBLEM #88

As hard as I try to maintain an optimistic attitude, I've become depressed by the job-hunting process. Am I doomed?

When it comes to landing a job, there is something far more important than keeping a positive frame of mind, and that is sending out your résumé.

You don't need a great attitude to function—you just need to do the work. Get out your résumés. Make your phone calls. Attend the networking events and mixers.

The key to true power is to honor and embrace all of your feelings. Don't squash down fear or pain in order to put on a happy face. But on the other hand, you needn't wallow in the drama of it all either. Of course it's hard when you come face-to-face with those moments in life when you know you are not in control, but the truth is, nobody ever is. You can hold on to a positive attitude—and be strung out much longer in your job hunt than you'd ever anticipated, and you can be depressed now—and get an offer for a job beyond your wildest dreams five minutes from now. This is not and never was your show.

When you are employed and things are going fine for you, it's easy to forget this. You become arrogant, lazy. You think your abundant life is a gift that rewards you for your goodness. The gift in this leaner period of time is that you are closer to seeing through the illusions now than ever before. This is your moment—your precious opportunity to peer through the crack of everyday reality and glimpse the great mystery. Nobody knows what is going to happen to them next. Good news—or bad? How could you be in touch with this and not feel fear?

Your mistake is that you feel that your fear means something bad about you. Will you be punished if you lose faith? Does acknowledging your fear invite the universe to give up on you? Do you have to believe in yourself to get a lucky break? Truth be told, if you surrender to the mystery, there is good news for you. For it is neither your positive attitudes nor your fearful ones that create your reality. There are forces at work in your life far greater than your moods and emotions. You cannot be good enough, work hard enough, be deserving enough, or think positively enough to ensure that you will get things to turn out for you just the way you want each and every time. In fact the most you can hope for is to positively influence the circumstances that fate hands you by walking the path of correct conduct. This you can do happy or sad, anxious or full of faith.

Persist in doing the everyday work of job hunting, and regardless of your mood at the time, you will pile up many small advances. Every day add to your reservoir. When you have piled up enough, you will tumble over the top, flowing effortlessly into what's next for you.

If you are putting off making your phone calls until you are in a better mood, see Tough Business Problem #47.

If you are scared that nothing will ever come through for you in your life again, see Tough Business Problem #97.

TOUGH BUSINESS QUESTION #89

I've always believed the fastest way to happiness is to have, do, and be the best. Now that I have, do, and am, why am I not happier?

Ask yourself, "Is my ambition driven by a desire to separate myself from others by standing above or apart?" However much you may achieve, only the success that unites with others carries with it the experience of fulfillment you seek.

You will invite happiness when you can turn your desire to achieve more than others into a blessing for them, as well as for yourself. You will be open to happiness when you feel grateful that the success of others can serve as an inspiration to you, even as you are grateful for what you, too, have already achieved.

This is an abundant universe. There is plenty enough for us all.

You have a choice about how you are going to relate to your ambition: Will you harden to protect or soften to receive?

If you need direction on how to soften to receive, see Tough Business Problem #93.

If you yearn for connection to your higher self, see Tough Business Problem #99.

TOUGH BUSINESS PROBLEM #90

I feel pressured to push myself forward all the time, to achieve more and more. I can never relax. Am I ever going to be able to find peace?

Unlike those individuals whose moods swing up when things are good, down when things are bad, you have found your own brand of stability. You are consistently anxious. Recognizing this is the first step toward the experience of relaxation you seek.

As things stand at present, you have gathered sufficient wisdom to understand that linking your inner experience to external reality is a losing proposition. Where your wisdom falls short, however, is that you have used this intuitive information to settle for the lowest common denominator: constant fear.

It's time to raise the stakes. By now you've probably tried stress-management techniques. Perhaps you've learned to breathe deeply and slowly, to close your eyes and rub your temples. But even the best stress-management tools will be little more than Band-Aids, giving at best temporary relief, if you don't recognize that the challenge you face is not just about pacing and technique but is at heart a spiritual issue.

To aspire to the experience of relaxation you seek, you will have to find that place within yourself that is always able to connect to wisdom, perspective, and balance, a place of inner stability that is large enough to encompass anything that fate brings to you.

Overachievers Anonymous is the recovery arm of the Society for Inner Excellence. Here is the Overachievers Anonymous Prayer that members of the Society for Inner Excellence use.

THE OVERACHIEVERS ANONYMOUS PRAYER

Help me to give up pushing, demanding, and desiring specific rewards from my work.

I trust that however confused and convoluted it feels at the time, I am always being led to my greater purpose the fastest, most direct way possible.

If it seems long and difficult at times, it is because I am a beginner and there is so much more to learn.

When out of my restlessness and frustration, I am tempted to take a shortcut I know does not come from my own desire for integrity, grant me the clarity to see that a fast, forced imitation will merely give the illusion of success.

When I am disappointed along the way, without anger, self-hatred, or judgment, I simply make whatever corrections I can. If I can't find anything to correct, or if I have reached the point where to give more will sacrifice my overall vitality and well-being, I have the patience to wait.

I ask you to help me love myself, wherever I am in the process, trusting that given who I am, where I've come from, and the circumstances I face, I am always doing my best.

When I am faced with deprivation—I will transform anger into gratitude for the daily practice that you have given me in the form of my job—a practice that is giving me the opportunity to send my roots down deep, the better to support the greater purpose you have in store for me.

AMEN

TOUGH BUSINESS PROBLEM #91

I've got a problem at work that's keeping me awake nights. The less I sleep, the less clear-headed I am. How can I ever hope to get a decent night's rest before the problem gets resolved?

When you've got a problem on your mind, your analytical brain keeps running programs looking for potential solutions, repercussions, worst-case scenarios, and so on and on. Telling yourself that you've got to stop thinking about the problem so that you can get some sleep has roughly the same result as telling yourself not to think about a pink elephant.

So what to do? You may not be able to stop thinking about the issue you are facing, but you can switch from thinking with your analytical left brain and tap into the inner resources of your spiritual-intuitive right brain. Your left brain's function is to process information; your right brain has the capacity to let things be. Your left brain works to keep control; your right brain can help you find an expanded perspective. In other words, your right brain can help you get some sleep.

Is there an efficient way to change channels from left to right?

Absolutely. It's called praying.

Praying rewires your mental circuitry, breaking up negative-feedback loops and letting you move on to deeper material. Often that deeper material takes hold while you are in deep sleep, in the form of dreams working out your problems on the subconscious level. Another possibility is that you drift into an apparently dreamless night, only to awaken in the morning with a fresh, creative solution on your mind.

Praying is an effective tool for business, one that should be required training for every MBA. (And before you laugh at this suggestion,

281

you should know that a vanguard of professors at the business schools at Stanford and Harvard universities, among others, have been experimenting with spiritual disciplines as part of an expanding arsenal of right-brain techniques with their students.)

Which prayer should you use? I suggest that you turn the light on, grab paper and pen, and write your own.

Following is a simple format, inspired by a prayer used in the twelve-step programs, that will allow you to start right where you are—with your left brain raging out of control—to refocus your energy in a more life-driven direction. You can use this format whenever the occasion calls for it, or experiment with prayers of your own.

Preparation for Life-Driven Prayer

First, answer these questions by filling in the blanks:

PART ONE

The biggest issue that is on my mind tonight is:

(a) _____

In relation to this issue, I feel I've:

(b) _____

    (State the problem, such as "made a mess," "failed," "run amok," "acted stupidly.")

When I think about this issue, the emotions I feel are:

(c) _____

    (Anger, shame, fear, etc.)

I refer to the Presence greater than myself as:

(d) _____

    (God, the universe, higher self, luck, etc.)

Now you are ready to write your first prayer. Take your answers from Part One and put them in the appropriate blanks.

My Life-Driven Prayer

Dear (d)_____,

This is me. These are my problems. Tonight I am particularly concerned about (a)_____.

In relation to this situation I did what I could, and I admit I've (b)_____. I feel my (c)_____about this situation and my part in it. I don't know what else to do about it. In fact I give up.

So, (d)_____, it's Your turn now.

I take (a)_____

and I take my (c)_____

and I place them in Your safekeeping, trusting that You will do what's best with them for me and for all concerned. I rest secure in the knowledge that, even as I sleep, You are working on possibilities for me that arise from outside my existing expectations and past experience. I am at peace.

AMEN

When you've completed your prayer, read it as many times as you need until you really feel the words and believe them. In the worst-case scenario you may be reading the prayer all night long. You will still be ahead of where you would have been had you spent the whole night lying awake worrying.

But the more likely outcome is that once you "get" the prayer, you will begin to relax, naturally and effortlessly. You will feel pleasantly sleepy. When that happens put down your pen and paper and turn off the light.

If your brain still wants to work, let your mind wander over the terrain of the prayer. Perhaps there's one phrase that really hits you. ("I am at peace," or "I place them in Your safekeeping," or "It's Your turn" are good possibilities.) Let yourself repeat it over and over as you drift off to sleep.

If you bring your best to praying and still can't get a good night's sleep, see Tough Business Problem #92.

TOUGH BUSINESS PROBLEM #92

I'm at my wits' end. I've done everything I know how to do and I've gotten nowhere. Help!

The more you are willing to challenge the status quo, the sooner you will arrive at the edge of your existing level of expertise and find yourself on new, strange terrain—often on both an external and an internal level at the same time. This humbling state is an indication not of what is wrong about you but of what is right about you.

Unfortunately, knowing this does not take away the upset you are feeling right now. You are used to making your way on your own, to navigating through familiar landmarks using the tools and skills that served you reliably in the past. You hate to admit that what once worked so well no longer works now. The last thing you want to do is admit this and reach out for help. But the *I Ching* warns that "if a man tries to hunt in a strange forest and has no guide, he loses his way."

Under these circumstances it is no disgrace to seek outside help: a business consultant, a therapist, a teacher, a friend.

"Bringing oneself to take the first step, even when it involves a certain degree of self-abnegation, is a sign of inner clarity. To accept help in a difficult situation is not a disgrace. If the right helper is found, all goes well," counsels the *I Ching*. "Neither false pride nor false reserve should deter us."

How does one go about finding "the right helper"? You are right to fear that when you expose your vulnerability to another, there is the possibility that you will give that person power over you. Your guide, in his or her professional guise, will appear wise and strong, while you are being forced to confront the very parts of your inner terrain that are weak and unformed.

The way to avoid giving away your power is to understand that no

285

matter how distressing the situation you find yourself in, you are seeking assistance in the matter out of choice, not desperation. You are on the hero's path rather than the victim's. You do not *need* to take drastic measures to ensure your survival. Rather you seek support and guidance on your courageous journey through life out of your strength and your humility. The difference is that *need* comes from fear, whereas the course you take is motivated by inspiration.

When you are inspired to seek help, you remember that your ultimate task is always to stay in close communication with and relationship to your own inner knowing.

Your consultant-teacher-therapist should never be someone whom you allow to come between you and your higher self. No one in that position holds the secret to your happiness. Rather the right guide for you will be someone who facilitates your coming into closer communication with your own inner wisdom.

Confucius teaches that the superior man knows strength and he knows weakness as well; "Hence the myriads look up to him."

If you are feeling frantic about your search for inner peace, see Tough Business Problem #96.

If you know you need help but you can't decide which of your many options to pursue, see Tough Business Problem #49.

If you are so excited about your therapist that you can't wait to tell all the people you work with about how much she could help them, too, see Tough Business Problem #40.

TOUGH BUSINESS PROBLEM #93

I meditate every day, but by the time I fight my way through the morning commute, I'm anxious and tense—and it goes downhill from there. Where am I going wrong?

The *I Ching* teaches us that the problem of achieving a quiet heart has occupied mankind since ancient times.

One way of achieving a quiet heart is through meditation. Meditation is a useful tool for educating your wandering mind to stay focused on the business at hand, whether breathing in the lotus position or typing out a report that requires concentration in a noisy office. By quieting your mind you can also make room for intuition and insight that would otherwise have gotten lost in the busyness that crowds the rest of your day.

But meditation, pleasurable and effective as it may be in its own right, can sometimes prove to be a fair-weather friend when confronting the realities of your daily life. The challenge is to take the lesson of a quiet heart, taught during your meditation practice, off the kneeling bench and into your office. The way to do this is to hold your meditation in a larger, life-driven perspective.

A more proactive approach to maintaining spiritual perspective may help you in this transition. The "Seven Steps to Inner Excellence," which follows, translates spiritual principles into action steps. These steps can be incorporated into your personal morning ritual along with your meditation practice. In addition you can refer to them periodically throughout the day, to reaffirm your faith when and where you need it most.

SEVEN STEPS TO INNER EXCELLENCE

1. I surrender the illusion that I can control everything that happens to me and to those I care about.
   I accept.
2. I place my trust in the universe, taking a leap of faith that there are forces beyond my understanding at work on my behalf every moment of my life.
   I trust.
3. I am willing to embrace all that I am—including my fears and limitations, realizing that to be fully successful, I must first be fully alive.
   I am willing.
4. I give my goals everything I've got, remembering that "everything" includes taking the time to nurture myself at a pace supportive of my overall vitality.
   I give.
5. I am now ready to ask for the fulfillment of my deepest desires. I share my requests, assured that the universe wants me to have all that I need to live a successful and abundant life.
   I request.
   (Here name three things that you'd like the universe to give you.)
6. I am receptive to possibilities that arise from outside my existing expectations and experiences.
   I receive.
7. I have the courage to do what's next, grateful that my ordinary self is enough.
   I am enough.

Should you choose to meet with others in a support or networking group, perhaps connecting with others in your community who have also joined the Society for Inner Excellence, you will find it inspiring and effective to work these steps in a responsive reading format.

Here's how. Select a volunteer to read the steps aloud. After each step the group affirms the step in unison by speaking aloud the bold-face response. When you get to step 5, go around the group, starting with the volunteer leader, with each individual asking for three things you'd like the universe to give to you. The group then affirms each request with the words "We hear you."

Whether you work these steps as a group or individually, "Seven Steps to Inner Excellence" will put you back on solid ground with yourself, boosting your ability to respond to any incident that your workday will present to you. No, things won't go your way each and every time, but if you assume that there are larger forces at play than your limited human perspective can possibly encompass, your anxiety and tension will recede.

You will be left with you, as you are at your very best. Devoid of delusions of grandeur, you will be as clear-headed and creative as is possible—and as is necessary to get the best possible outcome. You will have a quiet heart.

TOUGH BUSINESS PROBLEM #94

Spirituality is hogwash. Get real! What do you have to say to that?

You who call spirituality hogwash believe that you have a firmer grasp on reality than do the rest of us. Those among you who are "realists" portray spirituality as a kind of happy-face superficiality—a facile attempt to handle the challenges life presents with Sunday-school manners and a naive appeal to the goodness of your fellow man. Those among you who are "purists" mistake spirituality for the pitfalls of some aspects of institutionalized religion, believing that to bring heart and soul to the workplace is to foist one's personal beliefs on innocent bystanders. Those who are "self-made men" contend that you alone have the stuff it takes to make it on your own, while the weak-willed resort to spiritual imagery as refuge from life's aches and pains.

Among those "antsy" about spirituality in the business environment is Tom Peters, author of *In Search of Excellence* who recently wrote an article on his reservations that appeared in *Executive Edge,* a newsletter for business managers. In his essay titled "Spirituality in Business: A Negative Vote," Peters differentiates between "empowerment" and "spirituality." Empowered individual and organizational performance, according to Peters, has a quality of toughness, exemplified by the likes of the late Bill McGowan, chief of MCI, and former CNN president Burt Reinhardt. Empowered organizations are "largely a by-product of ethical, committed, spirited, joyous labor."

On the other hand, Peters portrays spirituality as corporate paternalism, a coddling of employees rather than demanding high standards of performance, all fed by facile spiritual talk better left at home than introduced into the workplace.

"When the talk turns to the spiritual side of leadership, I want to run," writes Peters.

"It should be enough if I work like hell, respect my peers, customers, and suppliers, and perform with imagination, efficiency, and good humor. Please don't ask me to join the Gregorian Chant Club, too."

Ironically I like Peters's description of empowered organizations and individuals. On the surface I find no discrepancy between the tough, hardworking, inspired corporate cultures he describes and the kind of mature spirituality that many proponents of new-paradigm business practice. In fact by his very description of some of his crankiest business heroes, Peters inadvertently reveals an appreciation for qualities that are, by their very nature, spiritual.

Peters says he "couldn't care less" if people he respects, such as G. E. boss Jack Welch, are deeply spiritual or not. But *spirituality*, according to *The American Heritage Dictionary*, is derived from the root word *spirit*, which means simply "the vital principle or animating force traditionally believed to be within living beings."

Few would disagree with the contention that you can't be empowered, tough, inspired, or any of the other qualities Peters admires unless you are a living being who has a vital principle or animating force within you.

The real issue is not whether we are spiritual beings but rather what beliefs do we, as spiritual beings, hold? Joseph Campbell taught that the beliefs you hold about the nature of business and of life will determine how you will manage your career. If you believe that this is a universe that rewards and punishes, you will be drawn to old-paradigm models of external authority. If you believe that this is a loving universe that wants you to succeed, you will be open to new-paradigm models that empower the individual.

Is this a dog-eat-dog world? Then business will be like war. Or is human nature essentially good and loving? Then the workplace will value communication and teamwork. Like it or not, we all believe something. But when you hold your worldview unconsciously, you become a victim of your beliefs.

The alternative is to bring your beliefs to consciousness through honesty and self-evaluation. Only then will you be able to choose the assumptions and beliefs that you ultimately adopt, which will color your decisions and behavior on the job and in your life.

If you choose to adopt the spiritual principles in this book and practice them in your workplace, you risk the misunderstanding of some—but you will have an extraordinary work life.

Creating a culture in which the individual is encouraged to tap inner resources, freeing him or her from the confines of arbitrary external authority, to make better business decisions, to find the most creative solutions and to take risks, is the expression of this spirituality—the very antithesis of corporate paternalism. Founding companies on an ethical and moral charter derived from a genuine desire and committment to serve the greater community is about giving expression to one's vital principle—not about lowering one's standard of performance. Sacrificing one's personal needs and desires in order to stand for something bigger than oneself is the result of mature spirituality—it is hardly about coddling oneself. And using words to reveal authentic thoughts and feelings and to share one's honest intentions requires one to scale the heights of spiritual courage and can hardly be called facile.

Part of Peters's quarrel with spirituality is that he, like many who have a negative reaction to the application of spiritual principles in the workplace, resists and resents the intrusion of organized religion in the workplace. But spirituality is not about Gregorian chant or missionary work (though of course it can include these religious expressions).

The real question concerning spirituality is whether you are willing to do the hard work, prescribed throughout the pages of this book, of becoming aware of your inner process—that is, bringing your unconscious beliefs into the light for consideration—of releasing those that no longer serve you, and of finding new and deeper ways of relating to your workplace, your life, and the universe.

Ralph Waldo Emerson contended that every individual has an essential choice to make: the choice is between truth and repose.

He who chooses repose "will accept the first creed, the first philosophy, the first political party he meets—most likely his father's. He gets rest, commodity, and reputation; but he shuts the door of truth.

"He in whom the love of truth predominates . . . submits to the inconvenience of suspense and imperfect opinion, but he is a candidate for truth, as the other is not."

If you choose love of truth over repose, you cut yourself loose from all moorings.

You are cut loose from conventional reality, but you come to respect the highest law of your own being.

You can't have both truth and repose at the same time.

Choose truth and you will embark upon the far more challenging path. You will often be fully engaged in struggle—with yourself, with the universe, and with God.

Yours will be a life of questions, not answers.

You will often stand alone.

Your path will take you into the void.

Often you will be surrounded by utter darkness.

You will know despair.

So why let go of safety and dive headfirst off the cliff into spirituality?

Because it is the way of being in life that opens up the greater range of possibilities.

If you sense that there's more to life than what you've already experienced—if you're beginning to understand that there's no use doing more of what didn't work very well in the first place—what's your alternative?

If you think people who believe in this stuff should get some serious help, see Tough Business Problem #40.

TOUGH BUSINESS PROBLEM #95

Part of me wants to go for success in the world in a big way—but part of me wants to take as much time and space as I need to develop myself spiritually. Which is better?

There is no universal answer. The real question is not Which is better? But rather How do I define spirituality? When you've answered this question for yourself, you will know what is right for you. The superior man can soar to the heights and play an important part in the world—or he can withdraw into solitude and develop himself.

We are taught by the *I Ching* that each one must make a free choice according to the inner law of his being: "If the individual acts consistently and is true to himself, he will find the way that is appropriate for him. This way is right for him and without blame."

What does spirituality mean to me? After several years pondering this question for myself, I came to the heartfelt realization that spirituality is simply that part of me that longs for fulfillment.

I experience the emotional color of spirituality as free-floating longing—a bittersweet yearning that I have come to value even more than what I used to call happiness. When my primary purpose was to be "happy," I invested much of my vital energy in protecting my fragile well-being from outside influences. I isolated myself from the dangers of intimate relationships by confining my interest in others to what they could do for me. I gleaned entertainment value from gossip—a competitive affirmation of my standing in the world by comparing success.

I worked hard—often to my ultimate detriment—to get the things in life that I thought would make me happy—things like houses, jobs, prestigious appointments. But since the "happiness" I got came to me from outside myself, it could also be taken away from outside. The happiness I once prized so highly turned out to be a fickle friend—present when the sun was shining, gone with the first sign of rain.

By tempering my happiness with spirituality, my relationship to others and to the world around me has deepened. I've expanded my emotional range to include a feeling of compassion and empathy for others. In short, I spend more time feeling pain—not only my own but that of the world outside myself. It is a state that I have come to think of as "fully alive."

Given that this is my experience of spirituality, I have now taken the path of self-development by throwing myself into, rather than retreating from, the mainstream of life. While I am often still pulled emotionally toward withdrawal from daily life, I have come to realize that for me such a stance has an element of escapism to it. I may always have the urge to protect myself; I must stay on my toes to make sure I do not misuse my spiritual pursuits in this way.

Although my fantasy is no less than to float freely in the nectar of connectedness to the universe—with no concerns, no obligations, no responsibilities other than to experience the love of the universe coursing through my veins—at present I have two children growing up in my charge, plus a husband, friends, and family who challenge me to grow spiritually by translating my universal compassion into acts of kindness here and now.

For the present I know that my job is to forage as best and as often as I can on the edges of my spiritual consciousness, bringing back the goodies I unearth for application in my life, and hopefully the lives of those I touch. While I do spend a fair amount of my time journaling, meditating, walking in nature, reading philosophical literature, I now do so from the perspective of developing myself in order to bring more of myself *to* the world. In short, I have discovered that there need be no discrepency between playing an active part in the world and developing myself spiritually.

And although I often comment upon the fact that if and when one brings spirituality into the marketplace, his or her career will blossom, the inverse is also true: Give yourself permission to bring your spirituality into the marketplace and your spirituality will blossom as well.

If you are disappointed that you don't have a vocation that reflects the depth of your spiritual calling, see Tough Business Problem #59.

TOUGH BUSINESS PROBLEM #96

I'm anxious to find peace of mind. I've bought fourteen books on the subject and received dozens of brochures for classes, but I feel overwhelmed. Where should I begin?

You bring the same ambition to your spiritual path as you do to your career. Can't you see how desire—even for something as noble as inner peace—easily gives birth to anxiety?

Your spiritual practice is simply this: Relax. Take your time. Spread out your books and brochures and just be with them. Sit quietly in their presence without opening a single page or reading a single word. Let them influence you by their very existence.

When you can feel calm—in one hour, one week, or one year—then you may reach out for one. Move your hand slowly toward the one that is calling out to you. If none calls out to you more than another with your eyes open, then reach out with your eyes closed. There can be no right or wrong in this. Trust your instincts. Reach out and make contact.

Bring this book or brochure to your heart and let it give to you. Do not open or read it. Rather sit quietly and feel its presence. When you can feel it giving to you—whether it takes one hour, one week, or one year—then you may open it.

Only when you have surrendered your ambition can you be trusted to read.

Now you are ready to begin. Begin anywhere—open the pages at random. Read a single word. A sentence. A paragraph. Read slowly and well. Appreciate the wisdom the words contain—not because of what they will do for you but because of all that you have within you to bring to them.

This is the way to finding peace of mind that will last not just one hour, one week, or one year—but forever.

If you are anxious all the time, see Tough Business Problem #99.

TOUGH BUSINESS PROBLEM #97

I got laid off after many years. My prospects for equivalent employment or income are dim. How do I keep my spirits up as I look for what's next?

The *I Ching* teaches that as long as man's inner nature remains inwardly stronger and richer than anything fate brings his way, good fortune will not desert him. For the superior man everything furthers—even descent.

At such a moment, when denied an outer role to play in the workplace, the superior man takes the opportunity to refine his character. The *I Ching* explains that he is like a well being lined with stone. True, the well cannot be used while the work is going on, "but the work is not in vain; the result is that the water stays clear. In life also there are times when a man must put himself in order."

During such a time he can do nothing for others, but his work is nonetheless valuable, because by enhancing his powers and abilities through inner development, he can accomplish all the more later on.

What kind of work is the *I Ching* talking about? The hard work of taking on a new challenge—an inner challenge beyond any you have undertaken in the past. "We should not worry and seek to shape the future by interfering in things before the time is ripe. We should quietly fortify the body with food and drink and the mind with gladness and good cheer. Fate comes when it will, and thus we are ready."

To be of good cheer—to give up worrying, pushing, and angst— is the hard work the *I Ching* asks of you. But how, you are justified in asking, can you possibly be serious about your life and your responsibilities and not be suffering and struggling to get out of your present dire straits and back to normal as quickly as possible?

The answer is found in the concept of duration. According to the *I Ching*, duration is the "self-renewing movement of an organized, firmly integrated whole.'' Before one can begin again, the end must be reached. This is done by an inward movement, by contraction. When the end is reached, this same movement turns into a new beginning, in which the movement is directed outward, in expansion.

In nature we see duration in the process of cellular division. We observe it in the metamorphosis of the caterpillar into a butterfly. We experience it every time we breathe air in and out of our lungs.

To withdraw from public life, whether by choice or by fate, and surrender to duration, does not represent a state of rest. Rather, duration represents creativity at its deepest levels—going *with* rather than *against* the times. When responding to a crisis such as the one you describe, giving yourself the time and space to nurture your spirit at the deepest levels is the fastest and most direct route back to the active, outer role you hope to regain in your life. This is the law of movement along the line of least resistance.

My friend John is a good example of this. I first met John when he was laid off from his job as an in-house management consultant with a high-flying manufacturing firm. He was depressed and anxious. A friend gave him my book *Inner Excellence* to read. He was so excited by the idea of relating spirituality to business that his first impulse was to ask me for a job. He flew out from the Rockies to meet me.

John's idea was that we would develop workshops to bring this material into corporations. It's a great idea, but neither he nor I had the funding in place. I was already engaged in writing this book, and he could not afford to invest the span of time and resources it would take to get something going from scratch.

He was deeply disappointed, but this time, buoyed by the spiritual principles of inner excellence, John refrained from self-pity.

While he continued his search for a new job, he also nurtured the passion that the idea of a spiritually oriented business workshop generated in him. Coming from a background in manufacturing, he was particularly motivated by his growing awareness of the connection between new-paradigm management principles and environmental concerns. There was no way of knowing how or even whether this idea would ever get off the ground, but John trusted his spirit, allowing himself to enjoy the chaos of inner creativity buoyed by faith.

As John networked for a job, he brought out his credentials as a management consultant for show and tell—but his enthusiasm flowed most freely when he shared his passion for transformation. In fact, along the way, while attending every business function he could get his hands on, he told just about everybody in Denver to read my book. He wrote about my work to state officials, top people in business, speaker's bureaus. He was single-handedly responsible for getting the book onto the best-seller list of at least one Denver publication.

He proceeded along these lines month after month—after month. I knew his funds would soon be running out. Finally I got a phone call from John.

He had taken things as far as he could—and there was still no firm job offer in sight. Every company he could think of had received his résumé. John had called them so many times that to call again would be bugging them. The phone was dead.

But he had an idea and he wanted my advice. Back in his high-flying days he'd worked up enough mileage to earn a round-trip ticket to anywhere in the world. What did I think about his taking off for a couple of weeks to visit Portugal? As it was off-season, he could stay there cheaply. Visiting Portugal was a lifelong dream of John's. But to leave now, in the middle of his job search, ran counter to every precept of contemporary success-motivation philosophy.

As I was inspired to share with him the story of the well being lined with stone, John made up his mind to go. He had done everything he could. Outwardly he had done the work of getting out the information that he was available for work. Inwardly he had exploded creatively, stirring up a lot of mud. Now it was time to let it settle.

I didn't hear from John after those two weeks in Portugal. In fact I didn't hear from him for several months.

Finally a letter arrived. It was a change-of-address form with a personal note attached. Upon his arrival back in Denver, one of the people to whom he'd recommended *Inner Excellence* had left a message on his answering machine. There was somebody John had to meet. That person turned out to be an environmental activist looking for someone who had not only the management-consulting credentials but the passion for transformation to take over the reins of a prestigious environmental organization and run it along new-paradigm principles.

It was a job that surpassed John's fondest dreams. He couldn't have imagined such a position—and yet, as he looked back at the year of his unemployment, it had been a job he had been training and preparing himself for all year long.

By enduring a period such as this lightly—rather than heavily—you give yourself optimum mobility. Like John you will stay alert, ready to notice and respond to the first signs of transformation—that the end has been reached by inward movement and has turned, as is the law of heaven, into a new beginning.

If you look around you and resent the fact that other people have kept their jobs while you've lost yours, see Tough Business Problem #89.

If you are at wits' end about being laid off, see Tough Business Problem #92.

If you feel your situation is hopeless, see Tough Business Problem #100.

If you can't keep a positive attitude, hard as you try, and you think this means you're doomed, see Tough Business Problem #88.

TOUGH BUSINESS PROBLEM #98

In following the spiritual path, I left my fast-track career to live a simpler life. Now I'm bored. What should I try next?

As long as you look to the externals of your life—be it the fast-track or simplicity—to make you happy, your spirits will rise and fall with your circumstances. Although you believe that your occupations have failed you, the *I Ching* calls yours a state of inner oppression.

You are looking for spiritual solutions, and you think the choices you make about your life will bring you peace and contentment. But the truth is that you are on dangerous ground when you use spiritual resources to quash your feelings rather than use your pain as an entree to confrontation and acceptance of the often bittersweet contradictions of living.

This category of inner oppression is called avoidance. Avoidance can take many forms:

- In the name of humility, you may deny the fulfillment of your vision by working beneath your true level of competence.
- In the name of growth you may move from one oppressive situation to another to avoid confronting the inevitability of pain as part of the human condition.
- In the name of surrender you may mistakenly confuse resignation or inertia with simplicity.
- In the name of self-acceptance you may lower your standards to excuse your own laziness.
- In the name of self-realization you may become selfish and self-indulgent.

In a state of avoidance you will be tempted to go to extremes because you will not yet have developed the stability of spirit necessary to sustain the inner qualities of character that are the prerequisite to success.

Where and how can you begin to develop a stable spirit? The place to begin is here and now, by feeling the pain of your boredom. Stay with it. Get to know it well. Even as you explore it, it will begin to change. The pain will soften and heal. Eventually, when it transforms into surrender, sweetened by the depth of your revitalized commitment to facing the truth, you won't have to wonder what to try next. You will already be fully engaged.

If you think you have to choose between success and spirituality, see Tough Business Problem #95.

TOUGH BUSINESS PROBLEM #99

I always feel like something's not quite right. How can I get rid of this cloud hanging over me?

Someone once asked Confucius, "Would you call a man who has succeeded in avoiding aggressiveness, pride, resentment, and greed a true man?"

Confucius replied, "I would say that he is a very rare person."

INVOCATION FOR INNER PEACE

I recognize my anxiety as yearning for connection to my higher self and to the love I know I am capable of giving and receiving.

Taking a leap of faith, I turn my attention away from what I am missing and look for opportunities to give to others.

I rejoice in the realization that I can jump into the river of love any moment I choose.

I do not have to have it all together now to be worthy of giving and receiving love.

For this most extraordinary purpose, my ordinary self is enough.

TOUGH BUSINESS PROBLEM #100

I've hit bottom and I don't think I have it in me anymore to try again.

This, too, will pass.

If everything's perfect and you feel like you're on top of the world, see response to Tough Business Problem #100.

Appendices

Index of Invocations

Write Your Own Life-Driven Prayer

Preparation for Life-Driven Prayer

First, answer these questions by filling in the blanks:

The biggest issue that is on my mind tonight is:

(a)_____

In relation to this issue, I feel I've:

(b)_____

    (State the problem, such as "made a mess," "failed," "run amok," "acted stupidly.")

When I think about this issue, the emotions I feel are:

(c)_____

    (Anger, shame, fear, etc.)

I refer to the Presence greater than myself as:

(d)_____

    (God, the universe, higher self, luck, etc.)

Now you are ready to write your prayer. Take your answers from Part One and put them in the appropriate blanks.

My Life-Driven Prayer

Dear (d)_____,

This is me. These are my problems. Tonight, I am particularly concerned about (a)_____.

In relation to this situation I did what I could, and I admit I've (b)_____. I feel my (c)_____about this situation and my part in it. I don't know what else to do about it. In fact I give up.

So, (d)_____, it's Your turn now.

I take (a)_____and I take my (c)_____and I place them in your safekeeping, trusting that You will do what's best with them for me and for all concerned. I rest secure in the knowledge that even as I sleep, You are working on possibilities for me that arise from outside my existing expectations and past experience.

I am at peace.

AMEN

The Good-Enough
Human Being's
Bill of Rights

1. Even if I fear that I am greedy, stupid, foolish, emotional, lazy, and bad, I deserve to have bosses, clients, suppliers, family, friends, and subordinates who respect me.
2. I have the right to protect myself from exploitation.
3. I can take a stand for myself and my beliefs and let the world march to the beat of my drum for a change.
4. I matter.
5. The universe loves and supports me—exactly as I am.
6. The universe has plans for me better than anything I've yet imagined for myself.
7. I trust in the universe and in myself and am grateful for all that has been given to me—as painful as it has been—because it has brought me to this moment.
8. I am a force to be reckoned with.
9. If you don't support my bill of rights with all your heart and all your soul and all your might, then clear out of my way.
10. I trust in the magic and miracle of my life, and no matter how sad and scary it is to leave the familiarity of being abused behind, I look forward with joyful anticipation to what's next.

Dialogue with
Your Higher Self

What situation in your life are you most eager to resolve right now?
What outcome would you most like to achieve?
How have you tried to resolve this situation so far?
What was it about this approach that did not work?
How do you feel about this situation?
What judgments have you made about this situation—or about the role you have played in it to date?
What payoff or benefit have you received from having this situation in your life?
What other way could you get the same payoff that would be better for you?
What is the truth about this situation?
What must you accept about this situation?
What can you change about this situation?
What would you like to see happen?
How would you be impacted if this situation were resolved?
What one thing are you willing to change to obtain the resolution you would like?

Reclaiming Your Projections

1. Think of a negative incident that has transpired between you and another individual that you would like to come to terms with. In relation to this incident what is the dominant negative quality that this individual embodied? Be as specific as possible.
2. Before you met this individual, who else in your life also carried this negative quality?
3. How have you expressed this negative quality in your life—either by doing to others, (or to yourself), the same thing you dislike about this individual or by bending over backward to avoid passing it on to others?
4. What do you secretly admire about this quality?
5. What good could come of admitting more of this quality in your life?

Seven Steps to Inner Excellence

1. I surrender the illusion that I can control everything that happens to me and to those I care about.
   I accept.
2. I place my trust in the universe, taking a leap of faith that there are forces beyond my understanding at work on my behalf every moment of my life.
   I trust.
3. I am willing to embrace all that I am—including my fears and limitations—realizing that to be fully successful, I must first be fully alive.
   I am willing.
4. I give my goals everything I've got, remembering that "everything" includes taking the time to nurture myself at a pace supportive of my overall vitality.
   I give.
5. I am now ready to ask for the fulfillment of my deepest desires. I share my requests, assured that the universe wants me to have all that I need to live a successful and abundant life.
   I request.
   (Name the things that you'd like the universe to give you.)
6. I am receptive to possibilities that arise from outside my existing expectations and experiences.
   I receive.
7. I have the courage to do what's next, grateful that my ordinary self is enough.
   I am enough.

Contributing
Sources

Alcoholics Anonymous. *Alcoholics Anonymous.* Alcoholics Anonymous World Services, Inc., 1987.
This is the book that taught me how to pray.

Anthony, Carol K. *The Philosophy of the I Ching.* Anthony Publishing Co., 1981.
Anthony provides a solid historical and cultural perspective from which to begin to familiarize oneself with this classic work.

Autry, James. *Life + Work.* William Morrow, 1994.
Autry's mission is to take spiritual principles and apply them in the mainstream corporate environment.

Boland, Jack. *Master Mind Goal Achiever's Journal.* Master Mind Publishing Company, 1992.
The Master Mind approach showed me a way to take philosophical principles and turn them into a proactive process. Inspired by this, I developed the material first introduced in Inner Excellence: Spiritual Principles of Life-Driven Business *into "Seven Steps to Inner Excellence." [The people of Unity, particularly Heidi Sherman and Scott Sherman, minister of the Unity Church in Palm Beach, Florida, have encouraged me in my work on this book from the beginning.]*

Boorstin, Daniel J. *The Creators.* Random House, 1992.
Profiles of heroic individuals through the ages, including Confucius, give just enough circumstantial detail to remind us that greatness has little to do with happiness, in the conventional sense.

Breton, Denise, and Christopher Largent. *The Soul of Economies.* Idea House, 1991. Hazelden, 1994.
"Economies don't exist for the purpose of driving up prices or garnering profits. They exist to serve the needs of humanity. In this activity, scarcity, just like risk, poses economic challenges, but it says nothing about how economies meet those challenges. That's for us to decide."

Chopra, Deepak, M. D. *Ageless Body, Timeless Mind.* Harmony Books, 1993.
Chopra is a welcome bridge between Indian mysticism and Western science.

Dominguez, Joe, and Vicki Robin. *Your Money or Your Life*. Viking/Penguin, 1993.
This book shows the way to living our lives so that our money is in the service of ourselves—rather than our lives in the service of money.

Emery, Stewart. *The Owner's Manual for Your Life*. Doubleday, 1982.
Through my early studies with Stewart Emery and Carol Augustus, I was introduced to the thinking of Abraham Maslow and Carl Jung. I was first posed a variation of the question "Is there a chance you're taking things too seriously right now?" in one of their "Actualizations" workshops.

Fields, Rick. *Chop Wood Carry Water: A Guide to Finding Spiritual Fulfillment in Everyday Life*. Tarcher, 1984.
This was one of the first books to popularize the notion that there need be no discrepency between spirituality and business.

Furlong, Monica. *Zen Effects: The Life of Alan Watts*. Houghton Mifflin Company, 1986.
"I am a mystic in spite of myself, remaining as much of an irreducible rascal as I am, as a standing example of God's continuing compassion for sinners or, if you will, of Buddha-nature in a dog, or light shining in darkness. Come to think of it, in what else could it shine?"—Alan Watts.

Gawain, Shakti. *Living in the Light*. Nataraj Publishing, 1992.
Shakti's affirmations laid the groundwork for my understanding that you can use words and emotion to invoke a genuine change of heart. Her honest descriptions of her life and her process as she walks the spiritual path are inspiring and instructive.

Giles, Lionel. *The Analects of Confucius*. The Easton Press, 1976.

Godfrey, Joline. *Our Wildest Dreams*. Harper Business, 1992.
"To change the system is a goal women have been engaged in from the time of the suffragettes. . . . Will we hang on to our values and discoveries and actually change the rules while insisting on a place in the game?"

Groves, Dawn. *Meditation for Busy People*. New World Library, 1993.
Simple, practical advice on meditation for the overworked. A good introduction.

Harman, Willis, Ph.D., and John Hormann. *Creative Work*. Knowledge Systems, Inc., The Institute of Noetic Sciences, 1990.
In addition to having written one of the seminal books introducing and legitimizing the concept of a new paradigm for business, Willis embodies the spirit of the I Ching *in both his writing and how he chooses to live his life.*

Jampolsky, Gerald G., M. D. *Love Is Letting Go of Fear*. Bantam Books, 1981.
"I claim my freedom by exercising the power of my decision to see people and events with Love instead of fear."

Kim, Richard. *The Classical Man*. Masters Publication, 1982.
While working toward my brown belt in karate, my sensei, Sam Samarrai, student of martial arts master Richard Kim, told me the story of the Australian crab. Through my studies with Zen Bei Butoku-Kai, I learned the secret of true power: the dynamic opposition of strength and relaxation.

Marrs, Donald. *Executive in Passage*. Barrington Sky Publishing, 1990.
"So you want to change your life? Well, the laws of ultimate reality will let you, but you have to be willing to move into uncharted territory for a while. . . . It is through the very act of overcoming the challenges and melting the fears that you will replace the old rules with the wisdom needed to create the new life you're looking for."

May, Rollo. *Freedom and Destiny*. W. W. Norton, 1981.
I am deeply indebted to Rollo May for weaning me from the myth that "you can have it all" and showing me the uses and value of limitation.

Naisbitt, John, and Patricia Aburdene. *Megatrends for Women*. Random House, 1992.
John Naisbitt has been the Paul Revere of the new paradigm—

announcing and legitimizing the application of spiritual principles in the mainstream corporate environment.

O'Brien, Paul. *Synchronicity.* Visionary Software. 1991.
An easily accessible version of the I Ching *on software. Through the electronic "casting of coins" the program can provide the opportunity to center and balance in the midst of the workday, without attracting undue attention. 1820 SW Vermont Suite A, Portland, Oregon 97219.*

Osterberg, Rolf. *Corporate Renaissance.* Nataraj Publishing, 1993.
"The primary purpose of a company is to serve as an arena for the personal development of those working in the company. The production of goods and services and the making of profits are byproducts."

Peck, M. Scott, M. D. *The Road Less Traveled.* Touchstone, 1978.
Peck's groundbreaking assertion that life is hard and you can't always do something about it introduced the concepts of both surrender and liberation to many of my generation. Through this book and subsequent works I learned to see addictions and anxiety as the yearning for connection.

Phillips, Michael, et al. *Simple Living Investments for Old Age.* Clear Glass Publishing, 1984.
I was introduced to this little book through Roger Pritchard of Financial Alternatives, Berkeley, California. As I navigate the challenges of midlife, I have been inspired to think of investment for the future in terms of engaging in experiences that cultivate character and passion rather than accumulating wealth at my own expense.

Ray, Michael, and Rochelle Myers. *Creativity in Business.* Doubleday, 1986.
Based on a groundbreaking course in the Stanford University Business School, this book is a rich resource sharing many new-paradigm tools and techniques for business people. The book introduces a process called the Basic Ten Questions, effective in moving people along the cycle of creative questioning. My "Dialogue with Your Higher Self" uses the Q-and-A structure to in-

corporate voice-dialogue work, Twelve Step material, and the I Ching *into a fourteen-question process.*

Senge, Peter. *The Fifth Discipline.* Doubleday, 1990.
To transform business, we must begin to think of ourselves and our companies as part of a greater system.

Shah, Idries. *Tales of the Dervishes.* E. P. Dutton, 1970.
This book contains teaching stories of the Sufi masters over the past thousand years. It was an oral Sufi teaching story that inspired the final response in my book. As I remember it, in the story a king asked for the secret to peace of mind. He was given a ring in a box but told not to open the box until the day of his greatest sorrow. One day his daughter died. Believing that he could not go on, he remembered the box. He opened it. Inscribed on the ring were the words "This, too, shall pass."

Stone, Hal, Ph.D., and Sidra Winkleman, Ph.D. *Embracing Ourselves.* New World Library, 1989.
Hal and Sidra's book and lifework have given us important new tools to access, understand, and dialogue with our inner voices.

Ueland, Brenda. *If You Want to Write: A Book About Art, Independence and Spirit.* Graywolf Press. 1987.
Brenda's sage book provides access to the creative process, as useful to the business person as it is to the writer.

Wilhelm, Richard, and Cary F. Baynes. *The I Ching.* Foreword by Carl Jung. Princeton University Press, 1950.
My most fervent hope is that you will be inspired sufficiently by my book to follow your heart to the source. I am deeply grateful for this book's guidance over the past twenty years—not only imparting to me a broad-scale spiritual education but also giving intelligent, specific responses to my personal inquiries.

Yutang, Lin. *The Wisdom of Confucius.* Modern Library, 1938.
An introduction to Confucianism.

TEACHERS

Gayle, Robin—Master of Divinity, MFCC, San Anselmo, Calif.
Robin is an extraordinary counselor on both spiritual and psychological matters. She runs an ongoing group providing guidance and companionship for women who are courageous enough to let go of the status quo to explore issues of descent.

Norman, John—Psychic healer and teacher, Corte Madera, Calif.
Through John, I learned protective and energy-channeling tools and techniques, including the rose square, shared in this book.

Rand, Yvonne—Goat.In.The.Road, 1821 Star Route, and Green Gulch Farm Zen Center, Sausalito, Calif. 94965.
Yvonne leads workshops teaching Zen practice. The long-walk-to-the-boss's-office walking meditation and the half-smile meditation are traditional Zen practices.

Temenos Associates—San Ansomo, Calif.
Temenos hosts workshops giving a broad-based introduction to a wide range of spiritual and psychological practices. I was introduced to the concepts of projection and voice dialogue at their Pathways II workshop.

Taking the
Next Step . . .

This book is just the beginning. You, too, can develop a personal, ongoing relationship with the *I Ching*. Carol Orsborn recommends the Wilhelm-Baynes edition of the *I Ching*, which is available in bookstores nationally.

If you would like to stay connected throughout the year with people on the cutting edge of the new paradigm, you can join Carol Orsborn's network of business people: the Society for Inner Excellence. Annual memberships include the monthly news sheet, *Inner Excellence: The Bulletin of Success and Spirituality*.

To join, send a check made out to Inner Excellence at the Society for Inner Excellence, P.O. Box 159061, Nashville, Tenn. 37215-9061.

Other works by Carol Orsborn, available in bookstores nationally, include *Enough Is Enough: Simple Solutions for Complex People* (New World Library, 1992) and *Inner Excellence: Spiritual Principles for Life-Driven Business* (New World Library, 1993). Her eight-tape workshop on cassette, "Fall in Love with Your Life: The 7 Secrets to Life-Driven Success," is available through Zygon International, 18368 Redmond Way, Redmond, Wash. 98052.

Carol Orsborn is available for speaking engagements and workshops. To arrange an appearance, call (615) 831-2790.